Hell with Everlasting Torments Asserted
By Nicholas Chewney

Hell with Everlasting Torments Asserted
By Nicholas Chewney

Edited and updated by C. Matthew McMahon and Therese B. McMahon
Transcribed by Beth Saathoff

Some language and grammar has been updated from the original manuscript. Any change in wording or punctuation has not changed the intent or meaning of the original author(s), and has been made to aid the modern reader.

Published by Puritan Publications
A Ministry of A Puritan's Mind
4101 Coral Tree Circle #214
Coconut Creek, FL 33073
www.puritanshop.com
www.apuritansmind.com
www.puritanpublications.com

This Print Edition, 2013
Electronic Edition, 2013
Manufactured in the United States of America

ISBN: 978-1-62663-055-0
eISBN: 978-1-62663-054-3

TABLE OF CONTENTS

MEET NICHOLAS CHEWNEY

By C. Matthew McMahon, Ph.D., Th.D.

Little is known about Nicholas Chewney (1610-1685). He was the minister of St. John the Baptist in the isle of Thanet, Margate and was ejected from his parish in 1661 for nonconformity. He was reinstated in 1662. He was a Reformed Minister and held to the doctrines of grace. Later he received his D.D.

He spent much of his time writing against Socinianism, and wrote 7 works, one which was a reply to Samuel Richardson in 1660 called, "Hell's Everlasting Torments Asserted." Richardson (a Socinian) wrote a pamphlet (in 1658) that attempted to overthrow Christ's doctrine of hell called, "A Discourse of the Torments of Hell...searched, shaken and removed." Chewney wrote against it, and thus we have the reason for the work in hand.

We know later that Chewney went to reside in Essex or Kent, and died in 1685. He was succeeded in his parish by a minister who referred to him as an able doctor of theology.

Two of his best known works are: 1) *Anti-Socinianism, or, A brief explication of some places of holy*

Scripture, for the confutation of certain gross errours, and Socinian heresies, and 2) *Hell, with the everlasting torments thereof asserted.*

[ORIGINAL TITLE PAGE]

Hell:

With Everlasting Torments Asserted

Showing:

1. *Quod sit*, That there is such a place.
2. *Quid sit*, What this place is.
3. *Ubi sit*, Where it is.

Being diametrically opposite to a late pamphlet entitled, *The Foundation and Pillars of Hell Discovered, Searched, Shaken, and Removed.*

For the glory of God, both in his mercy and justice, the comfort of all poor, believing souls, and the terror of all wicked and ungodly wretches.

Semper meditare Gehennam.

By Nicholas Chewney, M.A.

LONDON,
Printed by *F.M.* for *Theodore Dring* and are to be sold at his shop at the *Sign of the George* in Fleet Street, near *Cliffords Inn*,
1659.

INTRODUCTION

To the worshipful and his ever honored friends, William Parson, Esq. and Mrs. Dorothy Parsons, his virtuous consort.

Either of your names were more than sufficient for honor done to this small and weak piece in the patronage of the same. Yet, whom God has joined together, I did not dare to sever. To you both then do I make this application and dedication. Yours was the principal, and to whom else should pertain the interest? What you shall meet with in this treatise of vigor and solidity, I desire that you would entertain and cherish it. For it is yours; yours first in the birth and occasion and now in the nourishment and protection. What more languishing and abortive accusation given to the author; it's mine, like me, I'll father it. However, it will implore your charity, the charity of your fair interpretation, which if you shall safely hold onto, then you have nobly rewarded the endeavors of,

Sir,
Your most affectionate friend and servant,
N.C.

TO THE READER

What *anonymous* person tells you in the beginning of his epistle, you know to be true and will gratify him with a concession of the same, that what he presents there is both new and old. In other words, it is an old Originian heresy newly patched on the Socinian mast. In its reviving, that he may be indulgent to the creature, he does not consider how injurious he is to the Creator, whose mercy while he seems to magnify, he disparages his justice. For if there is no hell, no place of everlasting torment after this life (which he vainly endeavors to prove), not only the wicked—how loose and licentious in their lives, how profane and scandalous at their death—but also the devils themselves (who were reserved in everlasting chains under darkness to the judgment of the great day) may at last *be saved*. And how then will the infinite justice of God be satisfied, in which, as well as in his mercy, he will everlastingly be glorified?

I was once in the mind to have followed this bold undertaking *passibus aequis*, and to have set before you his ignorant mistakes, his willful errors, his false glosses, his fair pretenses, his foul purposes, his undervaluing the Scriptures, and his diminution of Christ and his sufferings. But I suppose these are already obvious to every judicious eye. I have then contented myself (and I hope you) with this downright confutation. In which, God knows, my aim in *aut praevenire erori, aut revocare errantem*; either to prevent a man before he errs, or to recall and recover him erring. It is a phrase often used by the apostles, "Let no man deceive you with vain words," (Eph. 5:6). *Nihil facilius est quam errare*, There is nothing easier than to err. There is no man that lives that does not err; sometimes in *via pedum*, often in *via morum.* That provision is very necessary for us because of κενοῖς λόγοις (*vain words*), especially in these bad times, when deceits lay as thick on the earth, as the grasshopper did on the ground in Egypt, that a man can scarcely set his foot beside them. But woe to those by whose pride and self-conceitedness the world is so filled and furnished with them.

Yes, but, some say, they urge the Scriptures for their opinions. So did Arius, Novatus, Aeruis, Montanus, Donatus, Pelagius, and the devil himself. Neither has there been at any time, any heretic so fruitless, that has not used the copy of their countenance; nor in any place any error so shameless, that has not been overcast with the blaze of these orient colors. Impostors make use of the Scriptures, to undermine those that desire to be guided by them, by their corrupt interpretations of them.

Yet it is no disgrace to the Scriptures that they are so depraved. It seems rather some grace to them, that Satan and his *imps* meddle with them. For by them they tacitly acknowledge that there is virtue and power in them. The bee gathers honey on the same stalk, from which the spider sucks poison. Some have been infected by their meats and drinks; yet either these things must nourish us, or nothing. Nor is it possible for impostors to find out a better color for their errors and heresies, then out of the Scriptures. Therefore, with that heavenly gold, they guild over their base metal, that it may pass the more current. But what they get by it they may put in their eyes and see near the worse; for they pervert the Scriptures to their own destruction.

Truly, I could wish that such impostors as these before they are suffered to meddle with the Scriptures, might be forced to put in sureties, that the sense they give of them should be sound and orthodox, and consenting with the church of God. For the trusting of every man on his single bond, to interpret any place of Scripture is the occasion of very much error, as we find by woeful experience. Therefore, they grow bold to utter their own fancies and look to be credited on their bare word. And what is this but *dominati fidei*, to lord it over the faith of others? Here it is, that the Scriptures themselves, which were by God ordained as a special means to bring us to the knowledge of him, by Satan's illusions become occasions of our more offending him.

As in dark nights pirates use to kindle fires and make great lights on the rocks and maritime coasts; whether, when the poor weather-beaten seamen steer in hope of harbor, they meet with nothing but wrack and ruin. So heretics flourish with the Scriptures, or at least some seeming flashes thereof, under the pretense of new, but false lights, to which, when distressed souls repair for succor, these pestilent seducers feed them with nothing but pernicious error.

This is the cunning point of these wicked impostors, something they will have you believe is good, to draw down the evil, the greater part shall be evil, to poison the good. *Miscent recta perversis*. But as the apostle from God, so I from the apostle, by the command of God, do warn you of these wicked perverters of the word of God, which come indeed in sheep's clothing, but inwardly they are ravening wolves, that you take heed of them, that you are not led, and so led away by them, lest you fall into the error of the wicked.

It may be that this counsel may be slighted by you, but they of whom I warn you, would give much, that such as I am, though now mean and contemptible in the eyes of the world, would hold our tongues and forbear speaking or would hold our hands and forbear writing against them. If they could procure (as who does not see that it's their great endeavor) our mouths to be muzzled, or our hands manacled by authority, or else delivered over to their wolfish cruelty; error would then play havoc, darkness would triumph, hell (though now divided) would make play-day, truth would languish, and all goodness would fall flat to the earth. From which sad influences, let every Christian pray, in that which was once the dialect of the church, good Lord deliver us.

HELL: WITH THE EVERLASTING TORMENT ASSERTED

There are three ways proposed by St. Bernard for our apprehending of divine things. The first is the understanding, which relies on reason. The second is faith, which relies upon the supreme Authority. The third is opinion, which relies on probability, *et veri similitudo.* Now there may arise in some men, some mistakings, some misapprehensions of the sense of some place of Scripture, there may arise some paradoxical imagination in them, and yet these never attain to the settledness of an opinion, they float in the fancy and are only waking dreams. Yet such imaginations, fancies, and dreams receive too much honor in the things and too much favor in the persons, if they are questioned or reproved.

By this means it comes to pass sometimes that that which was but straw at first, being blown by vehement disputations, sets fire on timber and draws men of more learning and authority to side with, and mingle themselves in these impertinencies. Therefore, it is good counsel that the wise man gives, "Answer not a fool according to his folly, lest he be wise in his own conceit," (Prov. 26:4). Every bewildered fancy that arises must not be so much as reproved, or called in question.

And though fancies grow to be opinion, and that men come to think, that they have reasons for their opinions, and to know that they have other men on their side in those opinions; yet so long as they are only opinions, of a little too much, or a little too little, in matter of ceremony or circumstance, as long as they are only deflectings and deviations on collateral matters, no foundation being shaken, no cornerstone displaced, as long as they are only pretermissions, not contractions; only contradictions, nor usurpations. They are not worthy of conviction, and there may be more danger than profit in bringing them forth into an over-vehement agitation. For those men whose end is schism, sedition, and distraction, they are brought near to their own ends and the accomplishments of their desires, if they can set other men together by the ears and make sober men to wrangle.

They must be opinions then, not fancies, and those opinions must have a contrariety, an opposition to certain truths. They must be held, maintained, persisted in, and published before it is fit to call them in question, or to afford them a confutation. A man admits an opinion sometimes to lodge in him so long, as that *transit in intellectum*; it fastens on his understanding, and that, that he only thought before, he now seems to know and believe. And then, *fides si habet haesitationem, infirma est*, as that faith that admits a scruple is weak: So, *opinion, si habet assertionem, temeraria est*, when that is only an opinion comes to be published and avowed for certain, yes, for a necessary truth, then it becomes dangerous; and that grows apace. For scarcely does any man believe an opinion to be true, but he has a certain appetite and itch to infuse it into others.

This itch, I suppose, has troubled this appetite stirred up and provoked a certain confident *anonymous*, in whom all these pieces meet and make up a body of error which he stiffly holds and publicly persists in; otherwise, I had never troubled either myself or the reader with this confutation; whose great endeavor it is to undermine and blow up hell in the belief of others because he himself is persuaded there is no such place. I have, therefore, set myself diametrically opposite to what he has written to that purpose, and in the management of this shall proceed by the consideration of these three *circumstances:*

1. *Quod sit*: That there is such a place of misery prepared and appointed for the wicked.
2. *Quid sit*: What this place of misery is.
3. *Ubi sit*: To satisfy (if possible) the curious inquiries of those who make the most question of it, I shall with as much light as the Father of lights has afforded me to determine where this place of misery and torment is.

THERE IS A HELL

First, that there is a hell; which place, though some think God never made, but that it grew out of our sins. Yet, it is manifest; it had a being even *before* sin, and that God made it before he had present occasion for it, or actual use of it. It was, without question, constituted before the angels fell.

Hell was framed before sin was hatched, as heaven was formed and fitted before the inhabitant was produced. For we must observe that God created angels and men after his own image—*ratione sapientes, vita innocents, dominio potentes*—wise, innocent, and powerful. But with all he gave them *flexibilem naturam*, a mutable condition which had power of standing and possibility of falling. Power to stand was of God the Creator; possibility to fall was of themselves as creatures. If God had given them an immutable nature, he had created them as *gods*, not creatures. Now out of the whole host of angels, he kept *some* from falling, and when all mankind was fallen, he redeemed *some* by his Son. As he shows mercy on some in their salvation, so it is fit that he should show justice upon others in their condemnation. And because there must be a distinct place for the exercise of the one and for the execution of the other, which are in God equally infinite, by an irrecoverable decree from the foundation of the world, a glorious habitation was ordained for the one and a terrible dungeon for the other. "And these shall go away into everlasting punishment: but the righteous into life eternal," (Matt. 25:46). So certain are both of these places that they were of old prepared for that purpose. "Come ye blessed of my [Jesus] Father, inherit the kingdom prepared for you from the foundation of the world," (Matt. 25:34), and "Then shall he [Jesus] say also unto them on the left hand, Depart from me, ye cursed, into everlasting fire, prepared for the devil and his angels," (Matt. 25:41). As God foresaw the different estates and conditions of men and angels, so he provided for them distinct and different places. So we know that such a place as hell exists, and that there *is a hell.*

First, the Scriptures testify plentifully, and that both in the Old and New Testament, though *Anonymous*[1] does not see it. But who is as blind as he that will not see? In the Old Testament, "The wicked

[1] Chewney will make mention of "Anonymous" which is really Richardson the Socinian whom he is writing against.

shall be turned into hell, and all the nations that forget God," (Psalm 9:17). If *Sheol* signifies the grave only, what punishment is threatened here to the wicked, which the righteous is not equally liable to? I am sure Mollerus was of another mind, who says: *The psalmist there declares the miserable condition of all those who live and die in their sins, Aeternis punientur paenis,* They shall be everlasting punished. And Musculus reads the place in this way, *Animi impiorum cruciatibus debitis apud inferos punientur, The souls of the ungodly will be punished in hell with deserved torments.* Also, "The sorrows of hell compassed me about: the snares of death prevented me," (Psalm 18:5). Some read the bands or ropes, for 'chebel' signifies both, but in the plural number 'cheblee' signifies sorrows as of a woman in travail. The word *Sheol* is translated as hell. *O siand. Pellican.* So the Septuagint reads the Greek word ᾅδου (Psa. 17:6 LXT), the ropes or bands of hell. And they so apply it first to David, *credebam me ob peccata mea inferno proximum.* I though sometimes by reason of my sins, that I was nigh to hell. So *Pellican* says the same. And what? Let it be that only this good man might justly fear the indignation of God, when he considered the heinousness of his impieties? Then to Christ, as prefigured in David, *qui peccatum et maledictum factus propter nos inferni dolores et cruciatus sensit. Who being made a sin and curse for us, felt those sorrows and torments of hell, which we had deserved.* So, Osiander also says, *videbar captus in laques inferni, et quasi in infernum detrudendus.* I seemed as taken in the snares of hell, as like one thrust down and detained there because of the burden of sin which lay upon me.

But if it is objected that this punishment and these sufferings and that death, which our Savior Christ endured, cannot be said to be eternal because they lasted only a time, which being expired, they were likewise finished. I answer that a thing may be said to be eternal two ways, either in respect of the substance, or in respect of the circumstance, the being or continual being of a thing in the former sense, Christ suffered eternal death, not in the latter. He suffered the essential part of those torments, which all the elect should have suffered to all eternity, though not the circumstantial in respect of duration. Besides, eternal death, in the phrase and dialect of the Scriptures, does not signify the perpetual dissolution of body and soul, as some understand it, for so the damned themselves do not suffer eternal death, but either the immeasurable greatness of infernal torments, or the everlasting continuance of the same. The first of which is essential, the other but accidental, that Christ suffered; this he could not, ought not to undergo.

He could not, because he is eternal *Life* itself, God blessed forever. *Amen.* He ought not, because it was his office, and his great undertaking in the same, to free us from death, by conquering the power and taking away the sting of it.

Lastly, Christ may be said to suffer eternal death potentially (if we may borrow that expression to declare our full and direct intention), though not actually; that is, *a death always enduring*, though not by him always to be endured. There is this proportion between that death which we should have suffered, and that which Christ suffered for us; the one being *infinite* in time, the other *infinite* in weight and measure. The Son of God then truly suffered eternal death in respect of the greatness of those miseries which he endured, and the sense of God's wrath in those sufferings which he sustained.

This may be more clearly illustrated, if we consider in which this eternal death of which we speak principally consists, which on all hands is acknowledged to be in these two things, namely, the punishment of loss, and the punishment of sense, both of which Christ our Redeemer suffered for us. Of loss, when being fastened to the cross, he was as it were, as least for a time, cast out from the presence of God and deprived of the apprehension of his favor, as appears by that sad complaint and doleful exclamation, which he made, "My God, my God, why hast thou forsaken me?" (Matt. 27:46). Nor are they competent judges of the condition of the Lord Jesus, who so sadly cried out, that say it was because God had left him in the hands of the wicked Jews, to use him at their pleasure. For many of God's servants have been exposed to the same malice and mischief, and yet never so passionately affected with it, as to cry out in the midst of their sufferings, that God had forsaken them because their enemies have prevailed against them. No, no, it was the sensible apprehension of God's dereliction that constrained him to break out into that dolorous[2] exclamation. Of sense, when he drank so deep of the cup of divine wrath, that he was sorely *amazed*, (Mark 14:33), and he himself complains that his very soul was *heavy unto death*, (Matt. 26:38).

---

[2] Sorrowful.

And in this sense, if there were no other, may we maintain that article of our creed, and in spite of opposition, truly affirm that Christ descended into hell. At which *Anonymous* shrewdly carps, and with which boldly quarrels, saying that these words are not to be found in the most ancient creeds, and so, would beat us with our own rod. But admit they are not, yet we cannot believe (as some do think and say) that they crept into our creed by *negligence*; for they did not come in as a great fire, or hand over head, but with grave advice and great deliberation were they inserted. And as Calvin says of them that they were received with the common consent of all the godly, and that there are none of the fathers, but do make mention of them, (*Institutes*, 2.16.8). So that it does not matter when, or by whom they were inferred, seeing there is nothing in them contained (setting aside some unnecessary interpretations of it), but what is consonant to the analogy of faith proposed to us in the most sacred word of God. And if the bitterness of some against them are such, that they will not suffer them to have admittance, Calvin, in the place before cited, undertakes to make it plain that there is so much of our redemption affected in it, that they cannot be omitted without an apparent loss of much fruit and benefit conveyed to us by the sufferings of our Savior, who in the working out of our redemption, underwent the heavy burden of God's wrath and felt those very infernal pains (as an effect thereof) which we had deserved, that we might everlastingly be freed from the same. So David speaking in the person of Christ says, *Angustiae infernales invenerant me*, "The pains of hell got hold upon me," (Psalm 116:3). Nor is it impossible, Mr. Willet says, to feel the torments of hell, though not in the proper place of hell. For the place considered in itself, conduces little to the suffering of the wrath and curse of God. Polyander says, *If Christ tormented the devils as they themselves complain in the land of Judea*, (Matt. 8:29), *then out of that infernal place, God could bruise Christ for our sins by the heavy weight of his wrath, in the same land, out of that place of torment, as he did, and is manifest by the prophecy of Isaiah*, (Isa. 53:10-12).

What contrariety then is among the learned, concerning the descent of Christ into hell, is principally in opposition to the papists, who affirm that he went down in soul actually to hell to deliver the patriarchs and the souls of just persons there detained in bondage until his death and passion. For, otherwise, it is fully agreed among them that Christ by *virtue of his death and sufferings vanquished and overcame hell and the devil with all the powers of darkness.* Willet says that this being taken for granted, that Christ by his descent into hell, shook the infernal powers and triumphed over them as is by some of our reverend fathers and learned brothers on great persuasion of many forcible reasons and arguments affirmed, is not by me impugned. So then I shall proceed.

Solomon says of the harlot, "Her feet go down to death; her steps take hold of hell," (Prov. 5:5). Where *Sheol* is translated as hell, and in the judgment of Lavator, is well-translated to *foveam vel infernum passus ejus tenebunt*, which he says is spoken, not so much of natural death, as of spiritual, and that eternal destruction, which follows upon it. And he gives this for a reason for so understanding the place. Whoredom, being an abominable sin, defiling the members of Christ, dissolving and making void the covenant between God and man, must be accompanied with an equivalent judgment, even excluding those that are guilty of it without repentance because no unclean thing can enter into the pure and undefiled kingdom of heaven. Mark the words, "But whoremongers and adulterers God will judge," (Heb. 13:4). If man will not,

God himself will and give them a portion of misery answerable to their transgression. To second this we read: *Nescit convivas tandem in profunda tartara deturbari, ut in aeternum cum impiis et sceleratis affligantur*, "But he knoweth not that the dead are there; and that her guests are in the depths of hell," (Prov. 9:18). So Lavator thinks this and it is well-translated by us that she does not know that the dead are there and that her guests are in the depths of hell. What can be plainer than this? And yet *Anonymous* does not see it.

That the Greeks translate *Sheol* into *Hades* is most true, but that *Hades* comes from the word *Adam* is far-fetched and very suspicious. Who would not rather conclude it to proceed from the Greek primitive particle, *non videre*, or *not to see*; or from ᾅδης, (*hades*) by reason of the darkness and obscurity of that place. And if the word hell is not (as he either ignorantly or impudently affirms) to be found in the Greek, I would have obliged to know how he would better translate these words of our Savior Christ: καὶ πύλαι ᾅδου οὐ κατισχύσουσιν αὐτῆς, "And the gates of hell shall not prevail against it," (Matt. 16:18). Beza and Pareus read it, *Portae inferorum non superabunt eam*. That is, says the one, *Quicquid consilio vel viribus potest satan, Whatever the devil by policy or power can bring to pass.* The other says, *Potentia aut machinae satanae, The strength or the crafty and subtle devices of the devil shall not be able to prevail against that church which is so founded upon the rock Christ.*

In the New Testament, the Pharisees having put a false gloss on those words of the Law, "Thou shalt not kill," (Matt. 5:21), our blessed Savior as the heavenly Doctor strenuously opposes it by his authority, "But I say unto you, That whosoever is angry with his brother without a cause shall be in danger of the judgment," (Matt. 5:22), teaching them, and in them us, that a simple forbearance of the real and actual slaughter of our neighbor is not sufficient to satisfy the strictness of that command, but that the violation of it is to be extended, even to the very heart and tongue. For, besides external murder there are three kinds of internal murder which are forbidden by the same, every one of which makes a man liable to the judgment of God. Now, as these three degrees of internal murder differ in weight, so he proportions a punishment agreeable to the heinousness of the same.

The first is rash anger against our brother, by which we are moved to an unlawful revenge; and for this allots the danger of judgment, declaring by it that took what punishment they in the Sanhedrin inflicted upon actual and apparent murders, they were liable to the same and did deserve at the hands of God, who were guilty of this secret kind of murder, being angry, even to revenge against their brother; which doctrine the scribes and Pharisees were altogether ignorant of, and did not, would not apprehend.

The second kind of inward or secret murder is to say to our brother, 'raca'. Which word in Hebrew is *Syriac or Chaldee*, it does not matter, we suppose, and there on very good ground, to be some apparent manifestation of a mind beyond measure incensed against our brother, by outward countenance, gesture, or motion, either of the mouth or hand, declaring thereby the rancor and malice that we have conceived in our heart against him; such a one our Savior says is in danger of the council. That is, contracts as great guilt to himself and is subject to as severe a judgment in the court of heaven, as any capital crime that is censured in the Sanhedrin, or high court of the Jews. For here again (as before) is an allusion to the great Sanhedrin, which took a cognizance of such notorious crimes as were committed, inflicted, and deserved punishment on such offenders for the same.

The third kind of secret murder is an open reviling and reproaching of a brother, for the word in use among the Hebrews not only signifies one bereft of reason, as we commonly understand it, but also a wicked and ungodly wretch. "The fool (so translated, or the wicked and willful atheist) hath said in his heart, There is no God," (Psalm 14:1). Now such a one says Christ, is in danger of hell fire. In which he again alludes to the great Sanhedrin and the highest degree of punishment that was inflicted by them, namely, to be burned in the Valley of Hinnom, which by a known metaphor is translated as hell itself, and the inexpressible torments of it. For as those poor wretches being enclosed in a brazen idol heat with fire, were miserably tormented in this Valley of Hinnom, so the wicked being cast into hell, the prison of the damned will be eternally tormented in unquenchable fire. This valley, by reason of the pollution of it, became execrable with the slaughter, blood, and stench of carcasses, that hell itself inherited the same name and was called Gehenna, of this very place. And that (1) in respect of the hollowness and depth of it, being a low and deep valley; (2) for the fire which poor souls here and the wicked there miserably sustain; (3) because all the soil and filth was cast into this place, and so are all unclean and polluted people in hell. To this last judgment of the Sanhedrin, Christ appropriates that kind of murder, which is by open reviling of a brother, that he might notify the heinousness of this sin, then which (more is the pity) none commonly is accounted lighter, nor more familiar. And that no man might justify himself, but that every man laying his hand on his heart may acknowledge that by evil will, rancor, and reproach against his brother. He has violated the commandment, and by it has deserved death and damnation in the judgment of God, as much as open and notorious murder did deserve condemnation in the judgment of men. The gloss that *Anonymous* puts on the words, by it to carry them to another sense and wring from them another signification is corrupt, and his reasons alleged to that purpose, not worth the answering. Again, speaking of that rich man, "And in hell he lift up his eyes, being in torments" (Luke 16:23). This he says is neither proof, nor the less because he says it; but why not? Because he says that it is a parable and not history. We have but his bare word for it; for Marlorate calls it a history, in which, he says, Christ describes spiritual things under such figures and in such terms as he knew would be most obvious to our capacity, and so best apprehended and applied by us. Besides, Tertullian *contra Marcion.* Hillary *in enar. Psalm 2.* Ambrose *on Lucian* and many others call it so. Now whether we will believe *Anonymous*, his single report and repute of it, or all these pious and learned authors in the joint issue concerning it, let the reader judge. For my part, I think it is no less than blasphemy to say that it is a fabulous and feigned story; for Christ, who is truth itself, did not use to sport with fictitious tales, to allure with vain promises, or terrify auditors with idle disguises, or fantastical appearances, as the poets of old in the fables of *Sisyphus, Tantalus,* and the Elisian fields, these were the whole host of heaven widened from the truth; but this of our Savior was most true.

Yet, grant it to be a parable; why then (Anonymous says) are we not to grant a doctrine on it? To which I reply, that the scope and proper intent of parables is either manifest and certain, or else conjectural and uncertain. If uncertain, then may not a doctrine by founded on them, unless we have some supply from other places of Scripture, for the clearer illustration and more firm confirmation of the same, and in this sense it is, as commonly affirmed. *Theologia parabolica non est argumentative*, Parabolical Divinity is not argumentative. That is to say, the scope of a parable is doubtful, as concerning those things which beyond the purpose are collected from the circumstances of a parable. But if the purpose and drift of a parable are apparent, why cannot some certainty be collected and something proved then, so we do not pass the bounds or wander from the purpose and the scope of it. The words then of Christ in this parable evidently declare that the souls of the faithful, immediately after they are separated from their bodies, are transported to a place of joy and happiness, and that the souls of the wicked so separated are cast into misery and torment. As for other things, which are but (as it were) circumstantially added, they are not, ought not, strenuously to be urged in proving doctrine of faith, seeing they serve for illustration only and make little to any other purpose.

Moreover, if all those places, which consist of figurative and parabolical speeches, are doubtful and uncertain, and so prove nothing; what certainty, I pray, may be gathered out of Scripture, seeing that very many and the very necessary and material truths in the Scriptures are parabolical and figurative?

1. If no doctrine may be built on parables, many excellent sermons of our Savior Christ, the great Bishop of our souls, were preached and penned in vain and to no purpose, which were spoken in parables to the people, and are in and under the same parables commended to us; but this is most absurd to think. And therefore that,

2. If all Scripture, given by divine inspiration, is profitable for doctrine, for reproof, for correction, for instruction in righteousness, (2 Tim. 3:16), then that Scripture which is contained in figures and comprehended in parables is profitable for doctrine and will also afford certain ground for the same. "For whatsoever things were written aforetime were written for our learning, that we through patience and comfort of the scriptures might have hope," (Rom. 15:4). All the reasons by *Anonymous* alleged to the contrary, not being worth one fig.

I will add one Scripture instance more and then draw to a conclusion of this first circumstance. "The same [speaking of those wicked ones which worshipped the beast and his image] shall drink of the wine of the wrath of God, which is poured out without mixture into the cup of his indignation; and he shall be tormented with fire and brimstone in the presence of the holy angels, and in the presence of the Lamb," (Rev. 14:10). We have here in this denunciation, or divine *anathema*, these particulars to be considered:

1. What is denounced, in other words, that they shall drink of the wine of the wrath of God.
2. The quality of this wrath, in other words, without any mixture of mercy.
3. The measure of it, in other words, a cup of indignation.
4. The effect of it, in other words, torment by fire and brimstone.
5. In whose presence, in other words, of the holy angels, and of the Lamb.

First, that which is denounced is that as they drank of sin, which was the wine of Babylon's fornication; so they should drink of punishment; wine for wine, but the wine of the wrath of God. It was sweet, though poisonable wine of which they drank first, but it shall be sharp and sour of which they shall drink next, and that most justly too because as the Lord looked for sweet grapes at their hands, (Isa. 5:4), who owned the Christian name and claimed the privilege to be of his church, but behold sour grapes;

therefore of such. Grapes as they gave to him, such wine he returns back to them, indignation and fury. "For in the hand of the Lord there is a cup, and the wine is red," (Psalm 75:8); and "For thus saith the Lord God of Israel unto me; Take the wine cup of this fury at my hand," (Jer. 25:15).

Secondly, the quality of this wrath, it is without mixture; in other words, of any mercy. So Ribera says, *non erat mistum divinis miserationibus*. There was a time when mercy might have been without any mixture of justice, which being neglected, now justice must be executed without any mixture of mercy. God has suffered much, and he has suffered long too; much in burden, long in continuance; he has not been eased by repentance. He is constrained to ease himself by his just vengeance. For though he suffers long in mercy; there is no reason that he should suffer always in justice. Mercy having had her time, justice must have hers also. Indeed, the cup that God gives to his own for their sins is full of mixture, as tempered by his medicinal and fatherly hand with the sweetness of mercies and comfort in the end, (Psalm 75:8), where it is far otherwise with wicked and impenitent sinners.

Thirdly, the quantity of it, it is a cup of indignation full to the brim, in which God seems to deal equally and proportionably with them. As they filled the cup of their iniquity, so he fills the cup of their misery. They shall see, yes, and fill it too, with what a proportionable analogy, their sinning meets with their suffering, whereby he manifests a very great difference between his punishing of the wicked in wrath, and the correction of his own in love, upon whom he will lay no more than they are able to bear, and whom He ever corrects in mercy and in measure.

Fourthly, the effect and operation of this direful and dreadful draught, the cup of the Lord's indignation, and that is misery and torment, and that in the highest degree, as of burning by fire, mingled with brimstone, as the jewel of it, which is found to be: (1) most obnoxious to the eyes; (2) most loathsome to the smell; and (3) most fierce in burning. Well therefore, he speaks of it, who said, *Facillime incenditure, pertinacissime servet, et difficillime extinguitur*. It is easily kindled, violently jeweled, and hardly (very hard indeed, which is never) extinguished.

Fifthly, their tormenting shall be in the presence of the holy angels, and of the Lamb. (1) Of the holy angels because in their sight they sinned, and in their sight they shall be punished. (2) Of the Lamb, against whom they sinned in siding with his enemies, while they professed themselves his followers. Therefore, says Ribera, *Ipsi magis crucientar, intelligentes se ab eo videri*. It is an addition to their misery, when they shall consider that he beholds them that was once slighted and condemned by them.

So, we see as clearly as if it were described with a ray of the sun that there is a hell, a place of torment provided and prepared for all wicked and ungodly wretches, and that plainly by Scripture proved. I know there are and have been many besides our *Anonymous* that have *vi et armis*, opposed it and wrangled against it. Danaeus reckons up nineteen several sorts of heretics that denied it. But, say what they will, the wicked would give much to be sure that the Scriptures in this particular were *not* true, *credere nolunt, et non credere nequeunt*; they will not believe, and yet they cannot choose but believe; truly their case is fearful.

The very heathen, though he denies it, has prescribed to the truth of it, that there is a hell, a place of torment for those that rebel against the gods, Homer (Iliad 8, not far from the beginning), *says:*

Where Jupiter speaking to the other gods concerning the Grecians and Trojans:

If any shall so hardy be,
To aid each part in spite of me;
Him will I tumble down to hell,
In that infernal place to dwell.

For *Tartarus obscurus*, was then, and so ever since, has been taken for hell, that place of torment appointed for the wicked. Also Horace, (*lib. Ode.*) speaking concerning Jove's thunderbolts, says:

Quo bruta tellus et vaga flumina,
Quo styx et invisi horrida taenari,
Sedes et.

With which earth, seas,
The Stygian Lake, and hell
With all her furies quake.

Nor was Virgil ignorant of it, when he *said:*

Dent ocyss omnes,
Quas meruere pati (sic stat sententia) paenas.

They all shall pack,
Sentence once past, to their deserved rack.

The horror of which place he acknowledges he could not express.

Non mihi se centum linguae sint oraq; centum;
Omnia paenarum perurrere nomina possum.

No heart of man can think, no tongue can tell,
The direful pains ordained, and felt in hell.

They ever retained so much light, as sufficed to make some discovery of that place of darkness; yes, some of them have been terrified with their own inventions concerning it and distracted with the sense of those very torments, which their own pens have described. As Pygmalion doted on his own picture, so they were amazed with their own comments. How much more if they had known those unspeakable miseries and intolerable horrors, as they are in themselves, and inflicted upon those damned spirits, that must forever undergo them? *Par nulla figura Gehennae*, Nothing can truly resemble hell.

Besides, many wicked wretches are punished, and many as wicked escape unpunished; now *justum est, ut qui partier peccarint, easdem paenas luerint*. It is fit that partners in sin, should not be parted in judgment. God does not punish all here, that he may show his mercy, in allowing some space of repentance; nor does he forebear all here, that he may manifest his justice, lest the world should turn atheist and deny his providence. *Parcit ut puniat, punit ut parcat*, He spares that he may punish, and he punishes that he may spare. He afflicts some in the suburbs of hell that they might never come into the city itself. But those evil persons, whom he suffers to pass on uncorrected here, he reserves to be condemned forever hereafter. Sin knows its doom; it must strike with pain either world, or in the world to come.

Yet further, in all things natural and supernatural, there is an opposition and contrariety. There is good; there is evil; light and darkness; joy and sorrow. Now, as there are two several ways, so are there two distinct ends. Heaven, a place of admirable and inexpressible happiness, where the good angels transport the souls of the saints, such as by a holy and rectified conversation have glorified God and adorned their profession. Hell, a place of horror and confusion, where the black and grisly spirits hurry the souls of wicked incorrigible and impenitent wretches, when they are once separated from their bodies.

Again, all men naturally honor the good and punish the evil. The Barbarians themselves have laws of castigation and instruments of execution to cut off irregular and exorbitant persons. And shall the great Creator come short in justice of his creatures and those Barbarians too? The law of nations requires that malefactors, if they escape with life, are banished forever. And shall not God banish such as have been rebels on earth, from his glorious presence in heaven, dooming them to that dreadful place of eternal torment? If this were not, *stabit cum nerone paulus*, Nero was as good a man as Paul; Esau should still have his birthright in bliss and Cain is a saint as well as Abel. As believers say, if in this life only we have hope in Christ, *we are of all men most miserable*; so might the wicked say, if in this life only we have sense of sorrow; we are of all men most happy.

Lastly, every prince is allowed this concurrence to his state, that as he has a pleasant palace for himself, his nobles, and his attendants. So he has a goal and dungeon for thieves and traitors. That heaven is glorious, where the great king keeps his royal and magnificent court, the outer side of whose pavements we delight to behold and admire the transcendent beauty of it. So is that hell a dismal dungeon, where he secures his enemies, the outside of which men are not permitted to have a sight of, lest they should be presently struck dead with the horror of the place. They that have seen the flames and heard the roarings of Aetna; the flashing of Vesuvius and the thunderings and burning flames evaporating from those marine rocks have not yet seen, no, not so much as the very glimmerings of hell. A painted fire is a better shadow of these than these can be of hell's torments and the miseries of the damned therein. Having then cleared our passage thus far, let us in sober terms ask *Anonymous* this question: Do you verily (whoever you are) believe as you write that there is no hell? *Quis daemonum ita credit*? What devil believes so? They know it and feel it, "And, behold, they cried out, saying, What have we to do with thee, Jesus, thou Son of God? art thou come hither to torment us before the time?" (Matt. 8:29). They knew torments were prepared for them and a time when these torments should be fully and fatally inflicted on them, and they were loathe to suffer before that time. Shall not men tremble to deny what the devils are forced to confess? What, eat, drink, and play, Epicuras; *Post mortem nulla voluptas?* No pleasure after death? None indeed to reprobates; there is nothing but hell for them, and they will find only a small pleasure in that. O, *Anonymous, Anonymous*, take counsel which the father gives: *Crede et fuge, credendo fugies;* believe and avoid it. By believing, you will avoid it. We are sure there is such a place; let us be only half as sure that we may escape it, and we will do well enough. Fear it so that we do not feel it. If we tremble at these torments while the wicked laugh and are jovial, we shall put off our fear of them; laugh and be merry when trembling and astonishment will seize upon them. "The king spake, and said, Belteshazzar, let not the dream, or the interpretation of it, trouble thee. Belteshazzar answered and said, My lord, the dream be to them that hate thee, and the interpretation of it to thine enemies," (Dan. 4:19). So may I say, let us from the bottom of our hearts repent, bewail our former iniquities, and believe the exceedingly great and precious promises of mercy, which God in Christ has set before us, and then the terrors of this place will not be terrible to us; the terrors will be to the devils who hate God and to the reprobates (his enemies that daily provoke God). For their tormenting cares, we will have flourishing crowns in the communion of saints and angels.

WHAT IS HELL?

And so I come to the next question, namely: *What is hell?* Though it was easier to inform the reader what hell is not than what it is, yet I will make the best discovery of it that I am able according to our first proposal. And if any complain of a need of method, let him know that the nature of the place admits of none. For who can speak orderly and methodically of that; *Quod nec modum, nec methodum novit*, that knows no method, keeps no order? And if any man expects an absolute description of this place, I excuse myself with that of the poet before cited, *Non mihi si centum linguae.* But as for Pythagoras's guest at the stature and pitch of Hercules, by the length of his foot; and we say in the proverb, *ex ungue leonem*, so by shadow and resemblance we may little conceive what is in sufferance. *It is then that place to which the justice of God confines reprobates for their eternal punishment.* The plagues there are external, internal, and eternal. External which consists: (1) in a privation of all comfort, a privative cause has a positive effect. Tully was banished from Italy, though the academy of the world was in Greece, and he wept bitterly when he remembered Rome. Exiled

Demosthenes, though he found much kindness among his enemies, would shed tears in abundance when he looked towards Athens. The captive Jews hung up their harps when they remembered Zion. Ovid laments that *Roma relinquenda est*, he must leave that famous and flourishing city, but when he considers *Scythia est quo mittitur*, he could not be comforted. It is the most unhappy part of unhappiness to remember former welfare. (2) In a sensible passion of universal anquish, the sight being punished with weeping, smoke, and the direful aspect of ugly devils and their damned crew; the ears with the dreadful howlings, horrid blasphemies, and horrible roarings of those miserable wretches who are now tormented there; the taste with thirst and hunger, even hot and dry, empty and unsatisfied; the smell with noisome scents and filthy favors; the feelings with scorching and burning, even as it were to the frying of the very marrow of the bones; yes, the whole frame and fabric of their once trimmed bodies shall be defaced and deformed, dull, heavy, and unwieldy, as a brand in a great fire, no part free from burning; such is the *extremity* and *universality* of those pains. Internal, that consists in a plenary desertion of God; they will be utterly deprived of his glorious presence in whose favor is life, and at whose right hand there are pleasures forevermore, (Psalm 16:11), but never to be seen or tasted by these damned wretches, nor shall they behold the sweet and amiable countenance of the Lord Jesus Christ or enjoy communion with his saints; but will be as continual sinners, so continual sufferers. Two contrarieties being reconciled in them, which otherwise would be impossible; the one extreme presumption, the other extreme despair. In presumption, for with bitter malice and a cursed heart, they will perpetually blaspheme and despitefully sin against the spirit of grace, (Rev. 16:11), also in desperation, without all hope of mercy or admitting one thought of peace; the one being a sin against the justice of God, the other against his mercy. Both of these proceeding from that sting of conscience which they continually feel, which is that worm which never dies. Eternal, not determinable with time, for then time will be no more, everlastingness will make their sorrows absolute. If all the lives (I say not men, women, and children only, but of all) and every one of the creatures that ever lived on earth or will live to the world's end, were all added to one another, and all spun into one life, this one life of these damned wretches exceeds them all. *Ubi per millia millia annorum cruciandi, nec in seculo seculorum liberandi*, says St. Augustine. *Myriads of years will not determine or put a period to their sufferings.* The gulf is so deep there is no getting out; *Ex inferno nulla redemption.* Therefore, it is called *Infernus, ab inferendo*, of casting in; for the wicked are so *cast in* that they can never be able to *get out*. As no *Habeas corpus* from death, so no *Habeas animam*, out of hell. That rich man in Luke 16 solicits his brothers; why did he not beg his own deliverance since he was able to have taught them by his own sad and woeful experience? O, he saw *ingentem haitum*, a vast, interposed gulf. He must leave that alone, and alone forever.

Those laments need to be comfortless, which afford to the distressed no hope of any kind of consolation; neither the comfort of mitigation. All hope of relief, (ἐλέησόν, *mercy* (Luke 16:24) is there denied, even to the drop of water to cool the tongue of the tormented, (Luke 16:24). Nor the comfort of liberation, no deliverance, no not at the last; for he is given to understand by reason of the great partition, their case is such, *Ut non possunt*, they can never look for any freedom there, (Luke 16:26), but must remain there in everlasting torments; so neither the comfort of relief *in*, nor delivery *from* the miseries of this place. Note the poor comfort, which in all the calamities of this life, still stick by us and never leave us. *Dabit dues his quoque finem*, an end will come. Here an end will never come; which is never deeply enough imprinted in us, nor seriously enough considered by us. That this will be and never have an end; and that *Cruciaris* will be *Cruciaris* forever and never decline into a past action tense is an exaltation of this sad contemplation and the greatest aggravation of their unhappiness, (Luke 16:25).

Now because it is the main design of *Anonymous* to overthrow (if it were possible) this truth, I will therefore fortify it with the greater strength and—I hope—prove by diverse and considerable arguments that all reprobates will be tormented with the devil and his angels, and that everlastingly, they will never admit either ease or end.

1. The Scriptures, setting forth the nature of these torments by diverse and emphatical expressions, evidently declare the same, as (1) per ὀδυνῶμαι, most exquisite pains, such for the suddenness and sharpness, as the pains of women travailing in childbirth, (Luke 16:24, 26); (2) per βασανισθήσονται, most miserable

tortures, such as are inflicted upon the most notorious malefactors, (Rev. 20:10); (3) per πληγὰς, most dangerous and deadly plagues, (Rev. 22:18). Then whoever is liable to and reserved for such pains, tortures, and plagues shall never be annihilated, but forever remain in and under the same. But the first is true of the wicked; and therefore, the latter.

2. The continued succession, or rather the perpetual continuation of hell's torments is notably expressed, (Rev. 14:11), which is the amplification of the former judgment, from the eternity of it; showing that it is such as will be both *easeless* and *endless*. "The same shall drink of the wine of the wrath of God, which is poured out without mixture into the cup of his indignation; and he shall be tormented with fire and brimstone in the presence of the holy angels, and in the presence of the Lamb," (Rev. 14:10).

He says that the smoke of their torment ascended up forever and ever, not (to speak properly) that there is any smoke in hell, because smoke proceeds from the resolution of matter, which by fire is consumed. Now if there were any such thing in the hell, it would be probable that the fire would sometimes be extinguished, but smoke here is either (1) a metonymy of the sign for the thing signified, as smoke is a sure sign that there is fire, and so the sense is that the fire in which they are tormented will remain forever, or (2) that with this fire, in which they are tormented is perpetual smoke and darkness so that they do not have so much comfort in it as a little light may afford; and this smoke will be a torment to them, if not equal with, yet not much inferior to the fire itself; and therefore, it is called the *smoke of their torment*, that is, the *smoke that troubles and torments them*.

And indeed it is only just, for as the smoke of their unrepented sins ascended first, by which God was sorely displeased and exceedingly provoked to take vengeance on them, so the smoke of their eternal torment should ascend next, to show that God had now given them *smoke for smoke*, (Rev. 20:10). And the devil that deceived them was cast into the lake of fire and brimstone. Here is set before us the full and final destruction of Satan himself, which may be called his second imprisonment forever in that infernal pit where likewise the beast and false prophet are and will be tormented day and night, which the very next words expound saying, "forever and ever," (Rev. 20:10), according to usual phrase, (Rev. 7:15, 14:11). For there is no vicissitude of day and night in eternity, nor is there any day in hell, but eternal night. This kind of expression is used to declare that those torments which the devils and the damned suffer there will be without any cessation or intermission.

3. The grace of repentance for sins past and amendments of life for the time to come are eternally *denied* to them; as the tree falls, so it lies. The door will be shut, (Matt. 25:10), the gate of mercy by which they might have entered will forever be shut against them. These chains can never be broken; if they were cords of wreathed trees of iron, they might be burst asunder, but the chains of vengeance never; besides, a great gulf interposes, by which they are forever disabled to pass to the habitations of the blessed. Now they to whom grace is forever denied here and the glory hereafter must necessarily be detained in misery to all eternity. The first is true of all reprobates and impenitent wretches; and therefore, the latter.

4. That infernal dungeon has no back door, no egress at all, "Verily I say unto thee, Thou shalt by no means come out thence, till thou hast paid the uttermost farthing," (Matt. 5:26), which can never be done to all eternity. Why then, those that are fast

bound in chains in such a place, out of which there is no getting, must abide by it forever. The first is true, and therefore, the latter.

But here it is falsely objected by *Anonymous. How does this stand with the justice of God, to punish temporal offenses with eternal scourges*? It was the rule of his own law that *paena non debet excedere culpam*, punishment must not exceed the fault, (Deut. 25:3). How can he then inflict eternal damnation for a momentary and temporal transgression?

I answer first that there is a double quantity considered in punishment; the one according to the intention of pain; the other according to the duration of time. In respect of the former, the quantity of punishment must be answerable to the quantity of sin, (Rev. 18:7); so much sin—so much sorrow; the more pestilent iniquity, the more torturing fire. For the other, we must not think that the continuation of punishment is limited with the continuance of the fact. Among men, adultery is only a short pleasure, yet often pursued with a long penance. But the duration of torment respects the disposition of the delinquent. *Poenae singuloum inaequales intentione, peonae omnium aequales duratione, Aquinas.* The pains of all are equal in continuance, unequal in grievance.

But secondly, and more particularly, I answer that it will appear to be more just, both in respect of the mind and intention of the sinner, of the matter in which he sins and of the person against whom he sins.

First, the mind and intention of the sinners considered, it will appear to be more just; for though the act itself, the sin committed, is only temporal and finite, yet the mind of the sinner is eternal and infinite; insomuch, that if he could live forever, he would sin forever; and therefore, as *Gregory* says: *Quia mens in hac vita nunquam voluit carere peccato, justum est, ut nunquam careat supplicio.* Because the mind of man in this life would never be without sin; it is just that it should never be without punishment in the life to come.

Second, if the matter and subject of sin is considered, we will find it to be of and in the soul; like the wounding of the body causes the death and destruction of the same, by reason of which there is no returning to life again, so the sin being the death of the soul, it must necessarily follow that it is perpetual and everlasting.

Third, sin, as it is a transgression of the Law of God, is much more heinous. As he that smites the prince, to whom principally and especially he owes his allegiance, more grievously offends, then he that strikes a private person. So every sin is of an *infinite nature* because of the infinite dignity of the person and his glorious majesty against whom it is committed; and therefore, it deserves an *infinite punishment*, which because it cannot be infinite, *secundum intentionem*, in the intention and greatness of it, it remains that it should be infinite, *secundum durationem*, in respect of the *duration* and *continuance* of the same.

Now further, the equity of God's justice in punishing the temporal act of sin with eternal torments, *Hugo* fitly illustrates by these examples; he says that, like as when marriage is contracted, *per verba de praesenti*, by words uttered in the present tense, though the contract itself, in respect of the ceremony of it is soon done, yet the marriage as the substance of it remains in force all the lifelong. So when the soul and sin are contracted together, it is no marvel that this contract holds as long as the soul endures, if it deserves everlasting punishment. And as where the fuel and matter of the fire continues, the flame still burns. So sin, leaving a blot in the soul, being the matter of hell fire, is eternally punished because there is still matter for that everlasting fire to work on.

In this way, then we see it is no injustice in God to punish sin eternally; he only rewards them whom he punishes, according to their works. For though the action of sin is temporal, *voluntas tamen peccandi, quae per paenitentiam non mutatur, est perpetua*, says *Gorrhan*. Yet, the will to sin, which is not changed by repentance, is eternal and perpetual. For the further description of hell, the Scriptures use three principal terms: the worm that never dies, the outer darkness, and the fire that cannot be quenched, (Mark 9:44).

First, the worm; this is not to be understand as a corporal worm, which if it were, would be terrible enough; for a man to live always dying and die always living with an adder sucking and stinging his vital parts. But we must know that after the world's dissolution, there shall remain no mixed body, but only man; no generation or corruption in the revived bodies. Therefore, this worm cannot be corporal, but spiritual, the stinging of a vexed, galled, tormented, and tormenting conscience. This, O, this is even *infernum in mundo*, a hell on earth; and consider, O, consider, *qualiter sentient in inferno*, what it shall be to their sense, who shall be tormented there in hell itself. It is so essential a part of their torment, that Christ Jesus makes a three-fold repetition of it in one, yes, at the close of one sermon, "Where their worm dieth not, and the fire is not quenched," (Mark 9:44, 46, 48). Great, yes, very great and inexpressible this punishment must be, which our Savior so often inculcates, within so small a space. The heathen poets made this one of these three furies which they fictioned to torment the damned.

Scindes latus una flagello,
Alter a tartaries sectos dabit anguibus artus.
Tertia fumantes incoquet igne genas.

One brings the scorpion which the conscience eats.
The other with iron whips the back flesh beats.
While the third boils the soul in scalding heats.

But if the testimony of a heathen will not pass for currant, or bear no weight at all with us, hear then what an ancient Christian poet *Prudentius* by name says to this purpose:

Praescius inde Pater liventia tartar a plumbo,
Incendit liquido, piseasq; bisumine fossas,
Infernalis aquae vurvo suffodit Averno,
Et phlegethontaeo sub gurgite sanxit edaces,
Perpetuis scelerum paenis obrodere vermes.

The prescient Father black hell burns,
With scalding lead and ditches turns
Into a flame, with sulfur mixed,
The internal streams rolling between;
And gnawing worms has put therein,
To torture wretches for their sin.

Some take this worm to be *recordation praeteritorum*, the remembrance of things past; and they are either sins committed, or good things enjoyed. Of sins, which will gnaw on their souls and bodies like a vulture preying on their hearts and will remember the former iniquities committed forever. Of good things enjoyed, *St. Augustine* observes that of the rich man's pleasure, *omnia dicit, Abraham de praeterito*, he speaks of all in the time past and gone. *Dives erat, vestiebatur, epulabatur, recipisti*; there was a rich man who fared, went, and received, all past and vanished away; all (like the counterpane of a lease) expired, or like wages received and spent beforehand. This *fuisse felicem*, the remembrance of what he had been must be a sharp corrosive to him so that for these poor rejected and damned wretches to remember the evils they have done is bitter. The good they once had is more bitter; the good they might have had is most bitter. Therefore, it is good counsel for us now, *praevide remala future, ne recordemur bona praeterita*, to foresee with fear the evil that will be hereafter, lest we remember with grief the good that has been heretofore. O, that our foresight was only half as sharp as our sense! Let us now consider seriously the pains that will be, so that we are never put to remember sadly the joys that have been.

Secondly, outer darkness, "Cast him into outer darkness; there shall be weeping and gnashing of teeth," (Matt. 22:13), which speaks of the unprofitable servant. But God did not make darkness, and whereas in the beginning of creation, it is said, "And darkness was upon the face of the deep," (Gen. 1:2). This was not a thing created, but a mere privation, or absence, not being of that light which was made afterwards. Nor do we think that this mist of darkness, into which the damned will be cast and tormented in hell, to be a positive thing; but as when the sun is hidden, darkness necessarily follows. So here, not any emanation of any beam of God's countenance, not a spark of his light comes into this prison of hell; therefore, where there is such a *privation lucis*, there must be intolerable darkness.

A good day makes amends for a bad night, but to this night belongs no day; it is everlasting darkness. The roughest tempest, the weariest journey, is not without some comfort because there is hope of an end, but these pains are endless in quantity as they are easily in quality. Joshua had a long day when the sun stood still in the firmament, (Josh. 10:13), yet that day had an end; the sun fell to its course again and at last did set, but here, the sun and moon will utterly cease to measure time by any motion. That is a long sentence that has no period; a doleful night which has no morning; a woeful darkness where no star will afford a glimpse; no taper to befriend it with light; yet, with such night and such darkness, God punishes all wicked and ungodly wretches that shun the light here—*clausi tenebris et carcere caeco*, in darkness and blind prison will they remain shut to all eternity.

Let us then decline the works of darkness, as we desire to escape this place of darkness and the darkness of this place. Inferior darkness must be doomed to inferior darkness. What is more just than they who refused the light when they might have had it? That they should be deprived of it, when they most desire it? There are too many of these among us, that nuzzle themselves up in ignorance, as if they meant to make their own beds in hell. Alas, it is a fearful place to take up lodging in, and so much the more fearful, by how much it is more than lodging, even an everlasting habitation. Voluntary blindness will be confined to necessary blindness; and they that might see now, if they would only open their eyes, will open their eyes there, yet they will not be able to see; to not see what they would, yet see what they would not, even to avoid the seeing of which, they would wish themselves to have no eyes. Now the God of grace and mercy, the sweet Father of lights, defend us from the prince, the power, and the place of outer darkness.

Last of all, unquenchable fire which our Savior mentions several times at the close of the sermon which we spoke of earlier, "...into the fire that never shall be quenched," (Mark 9:43-46, and 48), as if he could not speak enough of it, to terrify all that heard him about it that they might not be tormented in it, which continually burns the souls of the damned; and yet, it will never convert them into ashes. A fire indeed it is, but neither tolerable nor terminable. The breath of the Lord like a river of brimstone inflames it, and the breath of ten-thousand reprobates will never be able to blow it out. Scalding sulfur and burning stench universally will rack them; where heat follows smoke; and fire, heat; and stench; fire; and torment, stench; and the burning will be added to burning. The prophet puts that to question which is out of question, "Who among us shall dwell with the devouring fire? who among us shall dwell with everlasting burnings?" (Isa. 33:14). Surely, none.

I know *Anonymous* cannot get away with the word *ever* or *everlasting*, if it comes his way, and it will come. He endeavors to carry the sense of it another way that what is intended by the Holy Spirit. But he has very bad luck in it, for he exceedingly betrays his ignorance by it. He says that it is sometimes used for a limited time; therefore, it must always be so used (this is good logic). But let him give me one example where it is so used. Sin is like oil; as long as the oil lasts, the fire burns, and that is forever. If after so many millions of years, as there are drops in the ocean, there might be deliverance—there might be some hope. Alas, in hell there is no limitation, when the Lord shall give his being, they shall have ease, and not before. An infinite Majesty is offended, which these miserable wretches must forever undergo, unless some better informed and more merciful man, such as *Anonymous*, will get the keys of this place of horror, unlock the doors, and for mere pity, let him out of this place of torment. I know also, that it has been much opposed among the learned, whether the fire in hell is substantial or only allegorical. *Calvin* and some others are for the allegory, and they give this for a reason. There is mention of wood and of worm, as well as fire. Now the first two are allegorical; and therefore, the fire is also. But in Scripture, things spoken together are not always taken in the same nature and manner. As for example, Christ is called the Rock of our salvation; the *rock* is allegorical, so is our salvation allegorical? Likewise, our Savior says, "That ye may eat and drink at my table in my kingdom," (Luke 22:30). Eating and drinking is allegorical; therefore, is the kingdom allegorical too? For my part, I think we may safely conclude that there is true and substantial fire in hell, (Isa. 66:15). The Lord will come with fire to render his anger with fury and his rebuke with flames of fire. *Si in igne damnabit reporbos, quare non in igne crucibit damnatos?* says that father. *If he will judge the reprobates in fire, why not condemn them in fire?*

Grant it then to be substantial fire, yet, another question will be whether it is material, corporal, or spiritual. It is not material, for that kind of fire must be continually supplied and nourished with fuel. Yet, he that makes the damned live without food is able to maintain this fire without wood. It is not spiritual. Indeed, *Gregory* calls it an incorporeal fire, but it passes the nature of fire to be spiritual; yet, if with fear and without curiosity, we may look upon those flames, we may attribute a spiritual nature, to that more than natural fire. Though spirits have nothing material in their nature, which that infernal fire should work on; yet, such is the powerful judgment of that almighty Arbiter of the world, justly willing their torment that he can make spirits most sensible of those fiery tortures. And such is the obedient submission of their created nature that they may be immediately wrought upon by those appointed pains. And as this inspection cannot be with too much caution, no more can the conclusion that is drawn there from be with too much heed; for he that makes it spiritual fire only goes about to make it no fire at all. It is, therefore, by the consent of the many of the godly learned held to be corporeal fire, which being granted, there arise notwithstanding some exceptions against the same.

Objection 1: If it is corporeal, how can it diversely torment diverse reprobates? There is only one fire in hell, but yet, that fire does not excruciate and torment all the wicked, who are in it after one manner and measure; the more wicked men have been here, the more wretched will they be there. The mighty will be mightily tormented.

Response 1: For a better understanding of this, we know that this fire is the instrument of divine justice. Now, no instrument works only by its own virtue, after its own manner, and in its own measure. But it is regulated, ordered, and disposed according to the will and power of the first mover. The fire in a furnace is augmented or qualified, according to the will of him that kindles it, or has to do with it. So is this inflamed or mitigated by the power and will of God. "The breath of the Lord, like a stream of brimstone, doth kindle it," (Isa. 30:33). One and the same fire burns iron, wood, or straw, and that (as one well says) *secundum duritiem vel durationem materiae*, according to the nature of the incensed matter, is the rage and fury of the fire. *Gregory*, in the fourth book of his *Dialogues*, has a notable saying to this purpose: *Quod hic diversitas corporum, illic agit diversitas peccatorum, that which is wrought here by the diversity of bodies is wrought here by the diversity of sins.* One and the same fire may be common to all, yet, may it afford several degrees of pain to every one according to the pleasure of the great disposer.

Objection 2: If it is corporal fire, it must be maintained with fuel, or else it will quickly languish and be extinguished. But there is no fuel in hell, at least no such fuel as can maintain it to eternity. For *Anonymous* says that the wicked are compared to chaff and stubble, and so, are quickly consumed and come to nothing. But he will say that there are such because they are compared to such. Would he be contented that any man should infer because he (as a man) is compared to a beast that perishes; therefore, he is a beast? I suppose that he would rather reply, *nullum simile est idem*, for that similitude and identity are different things; as he that is like me is not myself. Indeed, man is compared to such, in respect of his fading condition in this life, but his mortal will, after, put on immortality. These bodies will be so rarified, as they will not admit of a diminution, much less annihilation.

Answer 2: We let him pass and answer that the bodies and souls of the damned shall be *loco carbonum et lignorum*, instead of fuel, and because of those materials (as they are qualified) are everlasting, it follows that hell fire must be everlasting also. For it is against the nature of fire to cease, as long as it has any combustible matter to feed upon.

Objection 3: If it is corporeal fire, then it is of the same species with our fire. Now, we know what the nature of the fire is, but not of that.

Answer 3: In the bodies, which are the matter of fire, there may be a difference, as *lignum igneum, et ferrum ignitum*, burning wood and burning iron differ; still it is fire, though diverse from ours in certain properties, which are unknown to us; and (if it is the blessed will of God), we may never know them. But seeing it is substantial and corporeal fire, it will not be amiss to take notice of some particulars wherein it differs from this elementary fire of ours, which may be considered in these *five respects:*

First, in regard to heat, our fire is hot; there is no element in the most extreme fury more afflictive to the sense than fire. But the fire of hell is far hotter and more afflictive. The fire in a landscape, which is *ignis pictus*, a painted fire, or that purgatory fire, which is *ignis fictus*, a feigned fire that has so warmed the pope's kitchen, are better representations of elemental fire, than elemental can be of that fire, which is eternal. That furnace, whose heat was sevenfold, (Dan. 3:19), insomuch that the flames of it licked them up, for whom it was not meant. The furnace was raging, very raging, and of great violence, but not a glowing sparkle compared to the everlasting fire of hell.

Second, in regard to light, our fire comforts in shining, but hell fire is oppressed with horrible darkness. *Ardet noster et lucet*, our fire burns, and in burning shines; but this, as divine *Justice* has disposed it, burns, but does not shine, unless it is for the greater torment of those that are frying in it. *Basil* says: *Vim comurendi retinet, illuminandi amisit*, it retains the property of shining. Therefore, it is called *Hades, sine sole domus*, a house without light. The apostle Jude calls it the *black darkness*. The darkness of Egypt was strong and horrid, so thick that it was palpable, yet nothing to the darkness of hell. In Egypt they had only an overcasting; they enjoyed the glorious light of the sun again. In hell, *non videbunt lumen in aeternum*, they shall never see light anymore.

Third, elemental fire burns the body only; eternal fire also burns the soul. The passion of the body is only the body of passion; the soul of pain is the pain of the soul; yet, if a consumable body is not able to endure burning flames for a day, how will an inconsumable soul and body be able to endure the scorching flames of hell forever?

Fourth, elemental fire, as it burns, consumes; hell fire rages more and wastes less. The reprobate shall have the punishment *uri*, to be burned, but not the happiness *exuri*, to be burned out. So when *Prosper* says *Poenae gehennales puniunt, non finiunt corpora,* hell's torments punish, but they do not finish the bodies. In hell there is no cessation of fire burnings, or of matter burned. The poet *Prudentius* speaks sadly of it:

Vermibus et flammis, summis cruciatibus avum,
Immortale dedit, senior ne flamma periret.

To worm and fire, to torments there,

No term he gave, they cannot wear.

If this fire were terminable, it might then be tolerable, but being endless, it must be easeless.

Lastly, our fire may be quenched, but the fire of hell never goes out. Our fire is maintained with wood and put out with water, but that, as it has nothing to maintain it, so nothing extinguishes it. All their weeping cannot mitigate the fierceness of those flames. And if there is any tears, they will rather be like oil that feeds it, than like water that quenches it.

The sum then is this: the torments of hell are comprised under fire because that is most violent and vehement of all the elements whatsoever. Water only kills; fire vexes, terrifies, and torments in killing. Yes, which is worse, this fire that never kills.

Let fools than solace themselves with a conceit that there is no such place. They will one day find it and feel it to their misery. Without a doubt it is good for us, *simper cogitare gehennam, always to think about hell.* And as we desire to escape the fire of hell, let us avoid the fire of sin. There are certain fiery sins that will find fiery punishments. Paul calls *lust* a burning sin. It is better to marry than to burn; who then would burn in lust here that fears to burn in hell hereafter? Rage and malice are burning sins; therefore, anger is called *excandescentia*, a waxing hot. They that nourish this fire within them are nourished for a worse fire without them. Blasphemy is a burning sin; let those whose mouths flame with oaths and whose tongues are set on fire of hell venting nothing but cursed speeches, fear these torturing and tormenting flames. Drunkenness is a burning sin; too much wine is the oil of hell's own lamp. They inflame the reckoning until they inflame their brains, inflame their blood, and inflame their bodies, and purchase as much sickness as comes to a burning fever and as much sin as serves to inflame their own hell. The entire world is on fire with sin, to make work for the fire of hell. And there is only one way to put it out: the water and blood that came out of the most precious side of the Lord Jesus. Only that water can quench the fire of sin in us here, and that blood quenches the fire of hell against us forever hereafter.

I might here enlarge this treatise with the consideration of the dire and dismal effects of these torments, which are principally two, in other words, weeping and gnashing of teeth, (Matt. 8:12). Rabanus says, Fletus *de ardore, stridor dentium de frigere*, weeping caused by the heat and gnashing of teeth by reason of the cold. This declares that there are these two extremes in hell—intolerable heat and incomparable cold. *Gregory* on Matthew 8 called therefore, *avernus absq, vera temperature,* where the freezing cold will not mitigate the scorching heat, nor the scorching heat qualifies the freezing cold.

It is observable that while we are here, the expense of tears outwardly mitigates and allays the sorrow that lies hard and heavy within and gives an ease to the surcharged heart. So the poet, *est quaedam flere voluptas,* the burden of indigestible grief (as it was) venting and emptying itself at the eyes; but hell by eternal tears could never yet qualify eternal pains. Besides, if we admit the weeping here, in the plain text, arises from the extreme perturbation of the soul and the horrible anguish of the body and may be said to be a howling like dragons than any true shedding of tears. Yet seeing one effect of the horrors in hell is weeping and such weeping as will never be comforted. Let us prevent our weeping there, by weeping here, where we may be comforted. The time of living is the time of repenting; if we die without repentance, repentance is dead to us forever. Weep then here and the time will come when God will wipe away all these tears from our eyes. For God has disposed *flentes ad risum, ridentes ad fletum*, weeping to laughing and laughing to weeping.

Gnashing of teeth is another effect of these tortures and arises from the sense of some sorrow mixed with indignation; a just and fit punishment that they who once gnashed their teeth at others should gnash their teeth at their own torments; they showed their teeth in derision, "There shall be weeping and gnashing of teeth," (Matt. 8:12). O, the dreadful horror and fearful terror of this sad and direful place, where there is neither help nor hope! No help; God will not, saints and angels cannot; nor would the damned themselves help one another, if they could. For they wish all others damned with them, then that they should be freed from them. No hope; men say in extreme passions, if it was not for hope the heart would break. There is no hope in hell, and yet, the heart must hold. It is a misery to these damned souls that it cannot break, even in a dying condition, yet without any hope of expiration. Seeing then there is no help, no hope of help in that place of torment. Let us seek help while we may have it and make much of hope that we may be enriched by it. The apostle tells us, "And hope maketh not ashamed; because the love of God is shed abroad in our hearts by the Holy Ghost which is given unto us," (Rom. 5:5); for if it could be issued, it would be ashamed. Now, if we would hope well, we must do well. He that tempts God does not hope in God; that hoping, thrusts all upon God and will out of a lazy devotion do nothing for himself. Many stretch themselves upon their beds as *Lepidus* in the shade and cry out: *O utinam hoc esset slavar!* But you know who said it, take that unprofitable servant and cast him into outer darkness. It is in vain for a man to hope to do well hereafter, as most men do, when he continues doing nothing but that which is evil here. The means must be used, where hope is nourished. Hope is only for the present; it has nothing in reversion. The saints in heaven have no hope, for they are in full possession of joy; the damned in hell have no hope, for they are in full possession of torment. Only the living have hope, and in the living God is their hope, which he increases here, that it may be comfortably consummated hereafter.

WHERE IS HELL?

The last question is *ubi sit*, where is the place of torment? I know that to rest within the bounds and limits of precedents is to overactive and to curiously inquisitive persons, a thing very contemptible; nothing is accounted wisdom with such, but what is exalted above the reach and pitch of those that went before us. To rest in positive divinity and articles confessed by all the churches; to be content to know that there is a hell, wherein tortures and torments are provided for the damned, and there is a heaven too, wherein salvation is prepared for the just and raise no estimation, no emulation, no opinion of singularity by the way, only to edify and not to amaze; only to bring men to an assent and to a practice and not to an admiration, is nowadays reputed but homespun divinity, made up only of human learning, so much decried so that they do not hold it necessary for carrying on the great work of instruction and edification.

Let us know (say these high-flown men) what God meant to do with man before ever God meant to make man; we do not care for that Law, which Moses has written, that every man can read, and that he might have received from God in one day. Let us know that *Cabal*, that which passed between God and him, and all the rest of the forty days. We do not care for God's revealed will, his acts of parliament, his public proclamations; let us know his cabinet councils, his bosom, his pocket dispatches. Is there not another kind of predestination than that which is revealed in the Scriptures? May not a man be saved though he does not perform those conditions, and may not a man be damned, albeit he performs those conditions, which seem to make sure his salvation in the Scriptures? How many miles are there between earth and heaven? And where is that very place that is called hell? Our country man, Mr. Holkot, upon the book of wisdom says well of that wisdom, which we seek in the book of God. All wisdom is nothing to me, if it is not mine; and I have title to nothing that is not conveyed to me by God in his Scriptures. And in the wisdom manifested to me there, I rest, as in other things, so in this, concerning the local being of hell.

Now the Scripture says, and that frequently too, this it is downward, "Let burning coals fall upon them: let them be cast into the fire; the deep pits, that they rise not up again," (Psalm 140:10); "But he knoweth not that the dead are there; and that her guests are in the depths of hell," (Prov. 9:18); and "The way of life is above to the wise, that he may depart from hell beneath," (Prov. 15:24). So the terms declare it, and the words describe it. *Sheol* is sometimes taken for a pit, sometimes for the grave, and sometimes significantly for hell, as we have already shown, all *downward. Mercerus* says about Genesis 37, that *Sheol* generally signifies all places under the earth; without a doubt it is below because it is everywhere opposed to heaven, which is above. It is, therefore, called the Abyss, a deep pit, a vast gulf, such a pit as by reason of the depth of it, may be said to have no bottom. The devils entreated Christ that he would not send them to this place, (Luke 8:31). *Beza* says in Matthew, *in abyssum* is *immensae profunditatis vorago, quasi absq fundo*, a gulf of an immeasurable depth.

The apostle that preached to the Jews used the word *Gehenna*, (James 3:6). Where speaking of an unruly tongue says that it is set on fire, a Gehenna, of hell, γεέννης. So *piscator*, that is, it is set on fire by the devil and that by a metonymy of the subject, as on the contrary, we find *caelum*, heaven, put for God in heaven, "I have sinned against heaven," (Luke 15:21). So hell is put for the devil. But *piscator* in James tells us that γεέννης is by the Hebrews corruptly called *Gehinnom*, that is the Valley of Hinnom. For so, in the time of Christ and his apostles, it was the place of the damned vulgarly called *infernus* and by profane authors is called *orcus*, and so indeed—as *Anonymous* affirms—the apostle spoke to them in a known dialect and used an expression that was familiar among them.

They also that preached to the Gentiles, when they spoke of this place, used the word *Hades*, which they then took (and sure they could not be mistaken) for a place of darkness and obscurity, wherein the wicked were everlastingly to be tormented. The apostle, speaking of the angels that sinned, says, "For if God spared not the angels that sinned, but cast them down to hell, and delivered them into chains of darkness, to be reserved unto judgment," (2 Peter 2:4). So *Beza*, in his annotations tells us what the Greeks called that place, which was ordained for the prison and torment of the damned. And reason itself teaches us that it must be opposite and contrary to that place, in which the spirits of just men made perfect reside which on all hands is granted to be above; therefore, hell must be *below*.

But against this it is objected that Dives in hell saw Abraham and Lazarus, which he could not do, if hell were so deep and so remote a place as commonly is affirmed. I answer, that albeit hell is below and downward in respect of heaven; yet (as some think) it may not be so in regard of earth. "Woe to the inhabiters of the earth and of the sea! for the devil is come down unto you," (Rev. 12:12), so that he was cast no lower than the surface of the earth. I know that there are diverse arguments on both sides. As they that live do not know the state of the dead, so the dead do not know the state of the living, much less of the saints in heaven.

But against this is opposed that if they in hell had not the sight of heaven, their own sufferings would less afflict them, for their most grievous torment will arise from the vision of what joys they have eternally lost. When they see it they will be tormented with terrible fear and be amazed at the saints' salvation. So *Bernard*, the faithful shall have a sight of hell and the reprobate a sight of heaven, *ut illi magis laetentur, videntes quid evaserint, et hi gravius erucientur, videntes quid manserint.* That the one may be more comforted by seeing what miseries they have escaped; the other the more afflicted, by seeing what happiness they have forfeited. "The wicked shall see it, and be grieved; he shall gnash with his teeth, and melt away," (Psalm 112:10). Bar then the sight of their eyes, and you mitigate the grief of their hearts. That weeping and gnashing of teeth of which our Savior speaks, (Luke 13:28), proceeds from sight; when you will see Abraham, Isaac, and Jacob, and all the prophets in the kingdom of God, and yourselves thrust out. It is their exile from the presence of the Lamb, from the society of the saints and angels, from the felicity and joys which they behold, that will most bitterly molest and trouble them, or else they could not be under the misery of that which is called *paean damni*, the punishment of loss. On the other side, it is said, that the sight of heaven is never afforded, no not to saints, but as a high, an inestimable favor. It was Paul's greatest grace and that which had like to have transported him beyond the limits of his holy profession, to be wrapped up into the third heaven, and to behold the life which the blessed live with God. But what extraordinary grace or favor is this, if it is also granted to the reprobates? The answer is easy; Paul saw that life and had a sight of those joys, *experiendo*, by tasting them and hoped again to see them *participando*, by a blessed partaking of them; such a sight is not permitted to the children of perdition. They see them to the grief of their hearts and terror of their souls that they cannot enjoy them, but are forever deprived of them.

But how could that rich man, spoken of in the gospel; or how can other damned spirits be said to see the glory of heaven, when as they want those luminary organs of the body, the disposition of sight; besides, the great distance between the several places and the thick darkness interposed? Which is a great question with *Anonymous*. I will easily remove this block out of the way, for even spirits see, though not with bodily eyes; they have the eye of intelligence and apprehension, by which they are able to distinguish matters of intricacy and perplexity, and that at a distance too; much more between light and darkness. They apprehend this glory either universally or particularly. They have a universal apprehension, whereby they perceive the saints to be in great glory; in particular, what this glory is, they do not know. They see it, and they see so much of it, as will augment their torment, *tam propter invidiam alienate faelicitatis, quam propter carentiam illius quietis,* both in regard of others gain and their loss; the transcendent happiness which the saints are forever made partakers of and their own want of the same. Now, if it is granted, that the damned will see the glory of heaven, then it will probably follow, that hell is in the air, only separated with a great impassable gulf, that either may not come to another. And I have read of certain hills whose tops have been so near one to another that men might talk one to another, but could not without many day's travel come one to another. If they do not see it, then it is as probable that it may be in the bowels of the earth. However, it is below, downwards, in the more inferior parts of the workmanship of him, who as the poet styles him, is *ille opifex rerum*, the great Creator of all. But to determine precisely whether in the air, or in the water, or on the face of the earth, or in the center of the earth, or in the center of the world's center, *Tegitur, non legitur, periculo se disquirirtur, tuto ignoratur,* it is kept secret and not discovered; it is safe to be ignorant of, but dangerous to dispute. That saying of *Scaliger* would be a seasonable curb to restrain us from a curious investigation and scrupulous inquiry after the place itself, if it were minded of us.

Nescire velle, quae Magister optimus,

Docere non vult, erudite inscitia est.

What the great Master will not have made known,
Our greatest wisdom is, to let alone.

Yet, thus far we may boldly conclude concerning it. That as just spirits separated from their bodies, presently ascend into the imperial heaven, there to possess joy and happiness, so the souls of hard, obdurate, and impenitent sinners, whose hearts neither the mercies of God could mollify, nor his judgments terrify, are confined below to the inferior elements, there to remain in everlasting miseries and torment. And this (as I take it) is, γένηται σοφός, to be wise to sobriety, according to the wholesome advice of the apostle. But to determine positively where hell is, and to measure out, and to dispose of every foot contained in the same, is audacious curiosity; and it is carefully to be avoided by us.

Now, because there is a difference among some that are more nice than wise about the *ubi*, *Anonymous* concludes against the *quod* to the betraying either of his ignorance, or infidelity, or both; because men will not be rash in it; therefore, such atheists will rashly deny it.

If any than shall ask further concerning the local place of hell, I answer with *Socrates*: I was never there myself, and my hope is that I never shall be; nor did I speak with any that came from there, and therefore, I cannot satisfy his curiosity. In this I confess many doubts concerning hell: *ubi sit*, where it is; none can describe *quid sit*, what it is; but all (all I mean in their right minds) do agree *quod sit*, that there is such a place, where the damned shall be imprisoned and in which tormented to all eternity.

KEEPING OUT OF HELL

Seeing then (as we have upon good reason concluded) that hell is a descent downwards; let us keep ourselves so far as we can from it, while we live that it may never devour us, when we die. Sin is a burden that presses downward. The prophet Zechariah compares it to a talent of lead, (Zech. 5:7); how heavy was it on the back of Judas? It never left him, until it had pressed him down to his own place. As the heaviest bodies drawn to the center of the earth; so do the saddest and heaviest spirits, such as the mercy of God has quite forsaken, draw down to the center of hell. Sin brings a man easily down, *facilis descensus averni.*

Things nearest heaven, take less care for earth; the fowls of the air neither plow nor sow, nor carry into barns. But men love most that which they must shortly leave and think seldom or never of that place, where they must, after the consummation of a short time here, abide forever. O, Lord give me the grace to consider the evil of my ways; *et simper cogitare gehennam, ne in gehennam incidam,* if nothing else will work me to repentance, to think often of hell here, that I may not fall into hell for ever hereafter.

The life of the damned is a death without end; the death of the damned is to live in eternal torments. When the wrath of God will cease towards them, then shall torments cease to be inflicted on them. But the wrath of God is *eternal*; therefore, their plagues must be eternal also. When those damned wretches will repent of their impieties, then they will be freed from their miseries. But the space of repentance was by them neglected, and the grace of repentance is now denied. Therefore, there is no deliverance to be expected. O, eternity, eternity, you alone add to and aggravate the punishments of the damned beyond all measure. Their misery is grievous in respect of the acerbity and sharpness of it; more grievous in respect of the variety and diversity of it, but most grievous in respect of the eternity and everlastingness of it.

Anonymous (how advisedly, and upon what grounds I do not know, for all his pretended reasons makes nothing to that purpose) says that this opinion (as he calls it) in other words, of the everlasting duration of hell's torments has caused much sin. I answer, how lightly he seems to set by it, by the term he puts upon it, it was a real and substantial truth before his cradle was made and will be so when his coffin shall be rotten. And if corrupt men will draw hellish conclusions from heavenly instructions, who can help it? Such bad consequences are not the legitimate children of God's sacred truth, but the bastards of man's own corruption, to whom they are to be brought and by whom to be fathered for their maintenance. I am sure, if we take a right course with it, there is good use to be made of it.

First, the glory and comfort of eternal life does more and more manifestly appear by this. This is a significant and delightful demonstration, which one contrary gives to another, when they are diametrically opposed. The day would not seem half so clear, if the departing sun should not leave night to follow it. The foil adds grace to the jewel. It (no less than) glorifies learning, that the malicious tongue of ignorance barks at it. He knows the benefit of heat that has felt the sharpness of a freezing cold. If there were no sickness to trouble us, health itself would not be precious to us. Even their opposition is an exposition of their nature. The consideration of the deformity and darkness of hell adds a greater and more glorious luster to the beauty and brightness of heaven, and those heavenly mansions which the merits of Jesus have purchased for the righteous.

Second, this doctrine (for so *Alstedius* calls it) is very necessary for the godly, that they may be moved in the serious consideration of it to acknowledge with the greater affection the mercy of God in Jesus Christ, by which they are freed from so great a misery, as this of eternal damnation, which we affirm (though *Anonymous* denies it, and by that, if there were nothing else to do it, *ex ungue leonem*, discovers what he is) that Christ our surety , in our place and stead suffered for us. And that is an undoubted truth, at which none but the children of darkness can take exception that which follows, will—I hope—sufficiently testify.

First, that prophetical speech of David where the grievous torments and infernal torments, which Christ our Savior sustained in the time of his passion, are fully and emphatically described; being such as no saint was able to undergo. And that the psalmist prophesies of the sufferings of Christ, and the psalm evidently declares the circumstances.

Secondly, the type and figure of it in the person of David, who by the instigation of wicked men, the sons of Belial was exceedingly troubled, and of which in many of his psalms he sadly complained, manifestly prefigured the future sufferings of the Lord Jesus, "The sorrows of death compassed me, and the floods of ungodly men made me afraid," (Psalm 18:5). Compare the same expression, "The sorrows of death compassed me, and the pains of hell got hold upon me: I found trouble and sorrow," (Psalm 116:3).

Thirdly, the description itself of the passion of Christ, what horrible anxiety he suffered in his soul; what consternation and contristation, in regard of those infernal torments with which he violently conflicted even to his death, for the sins of all the elect and the wrath of God due to them for the same, which lay so hard upon him that his sweat was great drops of blood, and an angel was sent to comfort him, (Matt. 26:36; Luke 22:43).

Fourthly, the surrogation of Christ in our place, forasmuch as he suffered instead of all the faithful, and all those things which should have been sustained by us, he in our place sustained for us: "Even as the Son of Man came not to be ministered unto, but to minister, and to give his life a ransom for many," (Matt. 20:28). Caiaphas prophesied when he foretold that Jesus should die for that nation, and not for that nation only, but also that he should gather together into one all the sons and daughters of God that were scattered abroad, (John 11:51-52; 1 Tim. 2:6); "For Christ also hath once suffered for sins, the just for the unjust," (1 Peter 3:18). But among all those things which he suffered for us, the chief was the infernal death, which by reason of our transgression was due to us, without which, all his sufferings had been to no purpose. And to this our doctrine tends, whatever wicked men think of it or speak against it; and therefore, confidently and comfortably affirm that Christ our mediator in our stead has undergone this also for us.

Fifthly, the reception and taking of our sin, which was by imputation laid upon him; seeing he has taken our sins upon himself and borne them for us, as plainly appears in Scripture, (Isa. 53:6; 2 Cor. 5:21). It is necessary also that he bear the punishment of the same; the principal part of which is this infernal death and condemnation, (Deut. 27:26).

Sixthly, the execration which he underwent—for he was made a curse for us, who were under the curse of the Law, (Gal. 3:13). Concerning which I have already declared myself elsewhere. Since then this curse infers that we were liable to eternal death and condemnation from which, Christ becoming a curse for us, did graciously deliver us. It is manifest that the death of Christ was different from the death of any, of all saints whatsoever, who in all their sufferings were neither made sin, nor a curse, nor were they forsaken of God, nor tasted the cup of his indignation; but were only fatherly chastised by him; nor did they wrestle with hell and the powers of darkness, unless it was, as with enemies already foiled, whom Christ by this death had vanquished and subdued.

Lastly, the confession of *Crellius* (and other of the Socinian brood to whom *Anonymous*, though he wishes well, must necessarily subscribe as not being worthy to carry their books after them) who says that Christ suffered death *instar maledicti a deo* (let him crack that nut); the effect of this must have been our punishment to all eternity.

We had spoken to this purpose before and had completed this argument, but that *Anonymous* would make the world believe that we are they that labor to overflow the sufferings of Christ, when indeed we are so far from overthrowing them and the sufficiency of it, by leaving any part of it unperformed by him, or to be completed by us that we rather magnify them, and his love to us, that undergoing such misery for us, we might by it be eternally freed from the same.

This is a truth, against which the gates of hell will never be able to prevail, much less the slight assaults of such poor and feeble undertakers as *Anonymous*, who, while he charges us with undervaluing the sufferings of Christ, does himself (by a Socinian trick that he has) undervalue the person of Christ by that corrupt gloss which he puts upon the words of Paul, "So by the obedience of one shall many be made righteous," (Rom. 5:19). He says that it is not by the obedience of God, nor by the obedience of the God-man, but by the obedience of one man (which word 'men' is not expressed in that verse, though it is with note of distinction, or opposition, in some verses before) are many made righteous. It is true—not by the obedience of God—for God cannot be said either to obey or suffer; but by his favor, by the obedience, testified both by the action and passion of that one person, which was God and man, many are made righteous. For the apostle there used the term "man" not understanding by it *hominem merum*, mere man, *sed hominem verum*, but true man. It was fit that the Redeemer of man should be true man, in regard of the justice of God, which could not punish sin except it be in that nature which had offended. It was fit also that he should be more than man, in regard of the heavy burden of God's wrath, which was to be sustained by him. The righteousness of whom, by which we are constituted righteous, is, therefore, by the communication of properties called the righteousness of God (*Mr. Downam* says), being the righteousness of that person, which is God as well as man. It is not the obedience of the Godhead; no, nor the obedience of the man-head, but the obedience of Christ the Mediator considered as God and man, by which we are made righteous.

I cannot, but by the way, lament the growth and insinuation of this pestilent heresy of Socianism, which under pretense of giving glory to Christ, robs him of all that true glory that belongs to him. It will allow him to be a holy, a thrice holy man, an irreproachable, an irreprehensible, an admirable, an incomparable man; a man, to whom, he that should equal any other man, was worse than a devil; a man worthy to be called God in a far higher sense than any magistrate, any king, any prophet. But yet he was no God, says this heresy and these heretics, no Son of God; a Redeemer by way of example, but no Redeemer by way of equivalent satisfaction. Paul says, "That at that time ye were without Christ, being aliens from the commonwealth of Israel, and strangers from the covenants of the promise, having no hope, and without God in the world," (Eph. 2:12). And he is as much an atheist still that pretends to receive Christ not as God, for if the receiving of Christ must redeem him from being an atheist there can no other way be imagined, but by receiving him as God, for that only and no other good opinion of Christ overcomes and removes his atheism. After the great day, whatsoever is not in heaven is in hell. He that then will be where the Son is now (if he is not in heaven) will be as far from heaven, as if he were where the center of the earth is now. He who confesses not all Christ, confesses no Christ. And this is the wickedness that keeps down *Anonymous*, and the rest of that heretical brood, that they cannot, will not, be raised up to the consideration of Christ as God. But we proceed.

The serious meditation of this doctrine restrains wicked men from their impieties: *Oderunt peccare mali formidine poenae*, Bad men for fear of pain do ill detest. The apostle says, "Or despisest thou the riches of his goodness and forbearance and longsuffering; not knowing that the goodness of God leadeth thee to repentance?" (Rom. 12:4); and well are they that will be led. But some that are that will not lead, with whom there is another course to be taken, such must be driven on whether they will or not. John the Baptist proposed the goodness of God as a special argument to persuade his hearers to repentance; do it, repent, and the kingdom of heaven is at hand, heard by you, (Matt. 3:2).

One would think this would have done it—have led them to it—but it did not stir them. He is fain to lay heaven by and the life, joy, and glory to come. And to betake himself to hell, to the anguish, tribulation, and torments there, for all these are in the verse under the words, "the wrath to come," so to drive them (if it may be) to it, since leading would not serve the turn. How strangely sin makes men dull and stupid that the kingdom of heaven does not work so kindly with them, as does the wrath to come? The loss of heaven, if that were all, would never restrain any from it; if no, *ira ventura*, wrath to come, they would never care for the loss of heaven. Repent, or you lose heaven; alas, this does not work any change or alteration. Repent, or you must go to hell, the place of endless and easeless torments that soon bites. This strikes fear in their hearts, and that brings forth repentance. So that this fear, even the fear of punishment, is good; though it is ignorantly condemned by some. It is true that the apostle says, "For ye have not received the spirit of bondage again to fear; but ye have received the Spirit of adoption, whereby we cry, Abba, Father," (Rom. 8:15). The spirit of bondage is inferior to the Spirit of adoption; yet, that spirit is better than the spirit of Belial, or that spirit of slumber, which the prophet mentions, whereby men's eyes are closed up so that they cannot see the judgments of the Lord, (Isa. 29:10).

It is a maxim that *actio perfecta non recipitur, nisi imperfecte primo*; there is no perfect action, but at first it is imperfect, and is perfected by degrees. It is a good thing to be a son, yet it is better to be a servant, "I had rather be doorkeeper in the house of my God, than to dwell in the tents of wickedness," (Psalm 84:10). It is good to be in Canaan, the land of promise, but (in the meantime), it is better to be in the wilderness than in Egypt. So fear and spare not, says *St. Augustine*; for *sinondum potes amore justitae, at timore poena*, Do it, if it is not for love of goodness, yet for fear of punishment. His basis is in Scripture, "O that there were such an heart in them, that they would fear me, and keep all my commandments always," (Deut. 5:29). Nothing brought the Jews to the love of God, but the terror they conceived of his judgments, which they visibly saw before their face; yet, God wished that they might have such a heart in them always, that they would so fear him; which for ought I can perceive from that place, was but a servile fear, procured by the terrible sights at the delivery of the Law.

There is no fear of God then, though it has some servility in it (so far as servility imports only fear of punishment), but is good; for *timor est amor inchoativus*, says *St. Augustine*. The love of God begins in fear, and then *amor est timor consummatus*, the fear of God ends in love. God often presents to us the joys of heaven, by it to allure us, but we have seen how coldly we are affected towards them; and therefore, as often the torments of hell, by it to terrify us from the evil of our ways. *Gehennae timor regni no assert coronam*, even the fear of hell gets us heaven, and we thank that pain which gives us sight. Though there may be a difference between *timor et tremor*, fear and terror, yet, the difference is not so great, but that they may both be found in and fall upon the best of men. When God talked with Abraham, a horror of darkness *fell upon him*, (Gen. 15:12). The Father of lights and the God of all comfort present, and present in an action of mercy, and yet a horror of great darkness fell on Abraham, the father of the faithful. When God talked personally and presently with Moses, Moses hid his face, (Exod. 13:6); he was afraid to look upon God. When we look upon God in those terrible judgments, which he has executed upon some and see that there is nothing between us and the same judgments (for we have sinned the same sins, and God is still the same God), what can we do, but stand in awe of him that we sin not.

He urges to prove this fear and sin, (1 John 4:18), but to little purpose. For the wise man says: *Timorem domini esse initium sapientiae*, "The fear of the Lord is the beginning of knowledge," (Prov. 1:7); and therefore, Jonah to the Ninevites, (Jonah 3:4), John the Baptist to the Jews, (Matt. 3:10), and all the prophets to sinners have used to provoke them to this fear by threatening the dangers that were imminent if they did not repent. But yet afterwards, when men are reclaimed from their iniquities, converted to God, and have made some progress in his service; then they change their fear into love more and more every day, until they arrive at last to that state whereof John speaks; which cannot be suddenly nor fully expected to this purpose. *St. Augustine* has a pretty expression to this purpose; he says that fear is the servant sent before, to prepare a place in our hearts for his mistress's love, who being once admitted into and possessed of it, fear departs and gives place to love. But where this fear never enters at all, it is impossible that love should ever take up a habitation.

And albeit, this fear of punishment is not in those that come up to that degree of perfection, which the apostle there speaks, nor is it less in them than in others; yet being joined with that reverence that becomes it. It is most necessary and profitable for such Christians, whose life is not so perfect, nor love so great. This appears by that of our Savior Christ, "Fear him, which after he hath killed hath power to cast into hell," (Luke 12:5). Also, Paul testifies of himself, "But I keep under my body, and bring it into subjection: lest that by any means, when I have preached to others, I myself should be a castaway," (1 Cor. 9:27); meaning by it, that notwithstanding all those favors, which he had received from God, yet he retained such a fear of God, as that he was careful in those relapses, which considered in their own nature, deserved exclusion out of those heavenly habitations, the glory of which in a very great measure, he has had some ocular demonstration.

Now (my friend *Anonymous*) if such a man as Paul did thus stand in awe of the justice of God, notwithstanding his apostleship, and those rare endowments, with which he was plentifully furnished for the execution and administration of the same, a man as holy as he; what should we be, whose consciences remains the guilt of many thousands of notorious impieties? *This know*, says the same apostle, "For this ye know, that no whoremonger, nor unclean person, nor covetous man, who is an idolater, hath any inheritance in the kingdom of Christ and of God," (Eph. 5:5). And, as though this had not been sufficient, he adds, "Let no man deceive you with vain words: for because of these things cometh the wrath of God upon the children of disobedience," (Eph. 5:6). As if he should say that those who flatter you in your sins, bolster you up in your iniquities, and say that God is merciful and easily won to pardon these or the like impieties—notwithstanding a delightful continuance—these men only deceive you;

for the wrath and vengeance of God comes on the children of disobedience for these very things. The author of Hebrews tells us: *Horrendum esse insidere in manus Dei viventis,* "It is a fearful thing to fall into the hands of the living God," (Heb. 10:31). The same apostle renders a reason: *Deus enim noster est ignis consumens,* "For our God is a consuming fire," (Heb. 12:29). They then who will not believe God's justice, nor are in any measure terrified with his threats against sin, but presuming his mercy and continuing in their impiety, will suddenly be surprised and irrecoverably confounded, when God's judgment seizes upon them.

Yes, but, Anonymous says, this causes melancholy and great trouble of mind. Truly, if we consider the condition that we are in by nature, we have a very small cause to be jovial. For, (1) there is a captivity wherein we are violently detained under the slavery of sin and Satan. Paul knew it and speaks of it, "O wretched man that I am! who shall deliver me from the body of this death?" (Rom. 7:24). I hope *Anonymous* will not be so foolhardy as to say that this trouble of the apostle was a sin, who being sensible of it, could only be troubled with it. Indeed, there is no Turk who so hurries his galley slaves and puts them in as base service as sin does to her captives. Give me one who has been in this captivity, and by the mercy of God is freed from it, *et scit quod dico*; he knows what I say is certainly true. And (2) there is a prison also. Ask David, who was never imprisoned, what he means when he says, "I am shut up, and I cannot come forth," (Psalm 88:8). What else could cause him to cry out so passionately, "Bring my soul out of prison," (Psalm 142:7). And Matthew says of some to whom Christ preached, "The people which sat in darkness saw great light; and to them which sat in the region and shadow of death light is sprung up," (Matt. 4:16). There are chains too, "And he shall be holden with the cords of his sins," (Prov. 5:22); "For I perceive that thou art in the gall of bitterness, and in the bond of iniquity," (Acts 8:23). And these are they for which David gives thanks to God, "Thou hast loosed my bonds," (Psalm 116:16). A man needs no other bonds, if once he comes to feel them. The gall that sin makes in the conscience are the entering of the iron into his soul.

But perhaps these are not felt by some; no, not felt? Take this then for a rule. If Christ heals them, those who are broken-hearted, broken-hearted we must be, therefore, he can heal us. He is *Medicus cordi*, the Physician of the heart indeed; but it is *cordi contriti*, of the broken-hearted. It is a condition that is always annexed to make us more capable; and likewise, it is a disposition to render us more curable. It is our fault, and a great fault it is, that we are more ready to laugh with the merry philosopher than to weep with the mourner. Mirth seldom knocks twice at our door without entrance, but sorrow will; and even with all the miserable helps that we can muster, we cannot keep it out. He who sees heaven lost, paradise vanished, earth accursed, hell enriched, the world corrupted, and all mankind defeated will have small cause to laugh. Man fell by affection of joy; he must rise again by the affection of sorrow. That part of the world which will be cast into the bottomless lake spends the days in laughter. That part which will rejoice forever must be first drowned in tears. For my own part, I am none of those who desire to go merrily to hell; I had rather have God's vinegar than *Anonymous*'s oil; God's wormwood than his manna; God's justice than his mercy; sorrow and mourning here than misery and torment forever hereafter. For a conscience troubled in itself is *odor quietis* as Noah's sacrifice was, a favor of rest with God.

Yes, but, he says, this opinion (for he will not allow any other term) provokes to despair. I confess that to despair of the mercy of God is sin of a very high nature. I have read of whole sects, whole bodies of heretics, that denied the communion of God's grace to others; I should see this, but not as frequent as some have imagined. The *Cathari* denied that any man had it, but only themselves. The *Novatians* denied that any man could have it again, having once lost it by some deadly sin committed after baptism. But I have read of any sect that denied it to themselves; no sect of despairing men. We have some, somewhere sprinkled; one in the Old Testament, Cain, one in the New Testament, Judas, and one in the ecclesiastical story, Julian; but no body and no sect of despairing men. Therefore, he who abandons himself to this sin of desperation, sins with the least reason of any; for he prepares his sin above God's mercy, and he sins with the fewest examples of any. For God has diffused this light with an evidence to all, that all sins (excepting that sin which is not without a great deal of difficulty, and some uncertainty defined as the sin against the Holy Spirit) may be forgiven to men, yes, to all men without exception.

But we must take heed, lest in magnifying the mercy of God, we decry his justice while we seek to keep some poor souls from dashing themselves to pieces on the rock of despair, we give no occasion to thousands to engulf themselves on the quick sands of presumption. And so we cast out one devil for another, and the latter proves the greater. Presumption is a sin to which we are naturally prone; and therefore, the more dangerous. Soon is a man invited to make much of himself, to approve and applaud his own endeavors, to look big upon his own performances, hardly won to his own affliction, or brought about to his own dishonor. Despair is a thing grievous to trembling nature. Not often does that archer of hell head his arrows with such displeasing assaults. Besides, this has often turned (*invito diabolo)* to a hearty contrition for sin and a holy conversion from sin, like a violent fever that has boiled up all the choler and corruption of sin so that a man becomes the better after it. But to presume is a sweet sin to flesh and blood that it once foiled innocence itself. Satan has not a more tried shaft in his entire quiver than to persuade men while they are sinning to bear themselves boldly upon the favor of God. Therefore, as the wise man eats moderately of the dish which he likes best because he knows that there is more danger of forfeit in that than in all the rest, so it becomes us to be more shy and heedful of that sin which we know will soon take us and take God from us. We may say of them both, despair and presumption, as the Israelite women did of Saul and David in their harmony after the slaughter of Goliath, "Saul hath slain his thousands, and David his ten thousands," (1 Sam. 18:7). So where despair has hurried some away with a great deal of noise and clamor, presumption has engulfed more, many more, without any noise at all.

Together with this sin of despair, in his linsey-woolsey discourse, he links the performance of holy duties. I know the devil and his instruments are protest enemies to it, but after that way which they deny, so will we worship the God of our fathers. The tree is known by the fruits; it is well said, *but well done faithful servant*, that by the mercies of God in the merits of Jesus we will gain acceptance and admittance. Has not God promised to reward every man according to his works? Has not Christ our Savior confirmed us by the same promise? And will this fellow make them liars? Does not the apostle enjoin the Corinthians to run that they may obtain, (1 Cor. 9:24)? Did not Jacob wrestle with Christ, the Angel of the covenant for a blessing and prevail? And how did he wrestle? As the prophet excellently expresses it, he prevailed by prayer and supplication, (Hos. 12:3-4). What is this, but with *Diogenes* to trample upon *Plato's* pride with more pride, to condemn our presumption (as he judges it) with greater presumption? For by this new divinity, or rather pompous language, he presumes to cross even the Lord Jesus Christ himself, who wills us to, "Ask, and it shall be given unto you," (Matt. 7:7). And James tells us that the reason why we have not is that we ask not, (James 4:2).

I think they should be ashamed to print and publish to the world that which is so apparently cross and contrary to the word of God, by it seeking to bring to men into a cursed condition, even to neglect and condemn the performance of those duties which we are enjoined to do in the name of the Lord Jesus. What will he, what can he say to that of the apostle, "Work out your own salvation with fear and trembling," (Phil. 2:12)? And "be ye stedfast, unmovable, always abounding in the work of the Lord, forasmuch as ye know that your labour is not in vain to the Lord," (1 Cor. 15:58). "Charge them that are rich in the world...laying up in store for themselves a good foundation," (1 Tim. 6:17, 19). "And, behold, I come quickly; and my reward is with me, to give every man according as his work shall be," (Rev. 22:12). Therefore, it is evident (notwithstanding his negation) that we may escape hell and do ourselves much good (though not yet) by our good works. Surely, after we have prayed for hallowing God's name, the coming of his kingdom, etc. We may pray not only for daily bread, but also for the pardon of and power against sin, and not to lose our labor. We are commanded to hear that our souls may live, (Isa. 55:3). For though God has promised and Christ has purchased all good things for believers, yet we cannot, not so soon at least, expect them, unless we seek them by those means which are appointed. See what the prophet says to the purpose that God has an intention of good towards his people, "I will yet for this be enquired of by the house of Israel, to do it for them," (Ezek. 36:37).

So, we see the Scriptures themselves are point blank for the performance of holy duties; but his intents are his purpose, his aim and his end is to undervalue the Scriptures by telling us that we have not the very books that were written by the prophets and apostles. Nor is it enough (he says) that we have books in Hebrew and Greek, unless we could certainly know that these copies (as they are called) agree word for word with those that were written by those holy pen-men.

To which I answer that if his ignorance is such that he does not know whether they are in accord or not, let him sit by and submit to the judgment of the learned godly. Let him not raise a dust to blind the eyes of others because he himself cannot discern truth from falsehood. But yet indeed, under a probable and plausible show of some learning, which God knows is very small, which is to presume strongly is none at all. Under the pretense of zeal and devotion, holiness and humility, labors obtrude his fallacies to the people, as sugared baits of serpentine deceit which he persuades himself cannot be done, but by endeavoring to overthrow religion, and the very basis and foundation of it, the Holy Scriptures. But that he may not outface us with a card of ten, we affirm, that the original text, the authentic Hebrew of the Old testament with the Greek of the New Testament, is entire and incorrupt; and for proof of this, do commend these ensuing arguments of the consideration of the judicious and Christian reader.

The first of this is drawn from the lack of proof on their side, who endeavor to lay so foul and imputation upon the Scriptures which they are bound to make good by some evident demonstration, but *hic* labor. They are a tree so firmly rooted that all the cold storms of humane reluctance and opposition could never shake. They then deserve, and that justly too, to be branded with a vain and profane suspicion of that for which they never yet, nor ever will be able to give a reason.

Secondly, from the testimony of Christ himself, where he says that one *jot or tittle* of the Law will not pass away, "For verily I say unto you, Till heaven and earth pass, one jot or one tittle shall in no wise pass from the law, till all be fulfilled," (Matt. 5:18); when it is manifest that God will not permit his word contained in the Scriptures, to suffer the least depravation.

Thirdly, from the incredible devotion, even to superstition, which the Jews bore to the Holy Scriptures; when it was enacted by them that if anyone should presume to change or alter anything therein, they were judged guilty of an unpardonable offense. Besides, if they would have done it, they could not; for it must have been done either before the coming of the Messiah or after. If before any such wickedness had been committed by them, they could not have evaded the just reprehension of Christ and his apostles; if after, the copies of it being dispersed among the Christians would have rendered such attempts vain and fruitless. And that they did not do it may appear by those places concerning the coming Christ in the flesh, which above all, and before all others would have been corrupted by them.

Fourthly, from the care and vigilance of the fathers, who have ever had recourse to and made use of these spiritual weapons against heathens, heretics, and profane persons, insomuch that no manifest depravation of the text could possibly creep in without public notice taken of it and as public clamor and scandal against it.

Fifthly, from the consideration that almost every age has afforded notable and famous critics, such as Origen and Jerome of old, Erasmus, Beza, and an infinite number of others in latter-times, who with a heroic industry and diligence, have weighted every tittle in the balance of the sanctuary and found it entire so that there cannot be any visible corruption found in it or apparent depravation of it.

Lastly, from the providence of God; if God could and would preserve the original and authentic

Scriptures, inviolate and propagate them to posterity; there is no doubt to be made but that they were preserved. But that God could, none can, none dare deny; that he would, in his providence, to the church testify to whom he so delivers his holy word that without any suspicion of error, it might receive instruction and information from it, "Lo, I am with you always, even unto the end of the world," (Matt. 28:20).

Now for translations, I confess that they cannot have that propriety, delicacy, harmony, and melody of language, which the Holy Spirit delighted in and made frequent use of, in the penning of the Scriptures. We know, that when the Grecians and the Romans and *St. Augustine* himself undervalued and despised the Scriptures because of the poor and beggarly phrase that they seemed to be written in, the Christians could say little against it, but turned still on the other and safer way, we consider the matter and not the phrase because for the most part, they had read the Scriptures only in translations which could not maintain the majesty, nor preserve the elegancies of the original. But however the Christians were at first fain to sink a little under that imputation, that their Scriptures had no majesty because those embellishments could not appear in translations with which the original did abound; yet now that a perfect knowledge of those languages has brought us to see the beauty and to behold the glory of those books and to come up so near to the same in our translations. Let a man that is endued with the spirit of discerning read the books in our translation, he will apprehend the author to be God; the matter to be divine and absolute that is in it contained, the manner and form to not be barbarous, trivial, market, or homely language, but as full of majesty as possibly could be rendered in the simplicity of words. And the end where they aim to be the glory of God alone may then conclude that these are the Scriptures and the very word of God. By the Scriptures themselves then in the original and by translation as near and agreeable to the original as the best and ablest expositors could possibly render them, have we proved that there is a place prepared, where all wicked and ungodly wretches will be tormented with the devil and his angels, and that forever.

Yes, but God delights not in the death of a sinner, (Ezek. 18), much less in the eternal damnation of any of his creatures. *Answer*: Yet, as mercy has had her place and day, so justice must have hers, whom mercy saves, she saves forever; though their works were short and nothing to God—yes—the very effects of his own grace. Therefore, whom justice condemns, she condemns forever; not so much respecting the person that has sinned, as the person against whom they have sinned: almighty God, as he is good, is not delighted with their torments; but as he is just, he is not satisfied without their torments. *Factus est malo dignus aeterno, qui hoc in se peremit bonum, quod esse posset aeternum* says *St. Augustine.* He is justly plagued with an evil that is eternal, who has corrupted himself in a good thing that might have been eternal.

But if God's justice must be satisfied on those sinners, for whom Christ did not satisfy, why is it not rather in reducing them to nothing? Seeing the unthankful deserve to be deprived of all benefits. Now one special benefit is being; therefore, *ipsum esse amittant*, let them not be. *Answer:* It is true, the creature that disobeys the Creator deserves to lose his being, but because it was given him to this purpose, that he should serve him; therefore, it shall never be taken away, for God will have his homage and service out of that very being, whether of grace and salvation to the praise of his mercy, or of punishment and confusion to the praise of his justice.

But *Anonymous* is of an opinion that the mercy of God will terminate their sorrows according to saying that you will have mercy on all and you love all the things that are, "For God hath concluded them all in unbelief, that he might have mercy upon all," (Rom. 11:32). *Sed conclusit et doemones*, he has also concluded the devils under sin. Neither will his goodness suffer that which he made for blessedness to perish forever in torment. Alas, these are only the plausible conceits that the over-merciful *Origen* first brought forth for the recovery of lost spirits; who, notwithstanding the doom of Christ, "Depart from me ye cursed into everlasting fire, prepared for the devil and his angels," (Matt. 25:41), would rather have these words, *minaciter quam veraciter dicta*, spoken by way of threatening than by way of truth. But the Scripture delivers it plainly, *ac plene*, "And the devil that deceived them was cast into the lake of fire and brimstone, where the beast and the false prophet are, and shall be tormented day and night for ever and ever," (Rev. 20:10).

Besides, this opinion does both *extendere et extenuare misericordiam*, as it strains, so it restrains mercy. It extends it to the future deliverance of the damned; it extenuates it in regard of the happy condition of the blessed. For if the lost are ever to be released out of hell, then it will follow that the saints are one day to be excluded out of heaven. And so, what the bad will gain, the good will lose; yes, the very mercy of God cannot get more glory by the one, than it shall lose by the other.

But though the devils are everlastingly chained up, yet there may be mercy for reprobate men that they may get loose, "And the Lord said, My Spirit shall not always strive with man, for that he also is flesh: yet his days shall be an hundred and twenty years," (Gen. 6:3). And he often threatens, but does not do, as we see in the case of Nineveh. Answer: God menaces many times and does not strike because our repentance steps between. But when everlasting burning has wasted all the moisture of repenting, will he do so for them? Here indeed we may speed as well as Nineveh did and find God in mercy inclining towards us, for we cannot choose but stand, as long as our sins fall; but we must fall, if our sins stand. But at that day, the date of repentance will be quite out of reach. Yes, but as David puts the question, "Will the Lord cast off for ever? and will he be favourable no more?" (Psalm 77:7). No, certainly, while there is life, there is hope; for that is spoken only of temporal afflictions, with which the Church is exercised while it is *militant* here below. But still as the joys of heaven, so the pains of hell are eternal. If they that say otherwise, *Anonymous*, and his gang can tell us when and at what time they shall expire, and then will they say something to the purpose.

For the conclusion of the whole matter, I think that God may justly say to *Anonymous*, as he did to that wicked and unreformable person, "But unto the wicked God saith, What hast thou to do to declare my statues, or that thou shouldest take my covenant in thy mouth? Seeing thou hatest instruction, and castest my words behind thee." (Psalm 50:16-17). It was fit and necessary that such men, before they are allowed to meddle with the Scriptures, should put in sureties that the sense which they give of them should be orthodox and consenting with the church. For the trusting of every man on his single bond, to interpret any place of Scripture, is the occasion of much error. So they grow bold to utter their own fancies and look to be believed upon their own bare word which is *Dominari fidei*, to take on them to be lords over the faith of others. If Satan comes to us in broad terms, charging us to renounce Christ, we should openly and utterly defy them; therefore, he creeps in like serpent, and as our Savior tells us *superseminat errores*, sows tares, (Matt. 13:25), that these growing together with the seeds of truth may in time choke them.

The things that were ordained for a means, whereby the Gentiles might come to know God by Satan's illusion became occasions of their more offending him, (Rom. 1:20). By the visible things of the creation, they might have understood the invisible things of the Godhead. But they fell to worship the sun, moon, and creatures, omitting the knowledge of the Creator. Where should we know Christ, but in and by the Scriptures? "Search the scriptures; for in them ye think ye have eternal life: and they are they which testify of me," (John 5:39). Yet as it often happens, that in the very highway we cannot see for dust, so on the face of this sacred spring, the devil collects such clouds of errors that many men do lose Christ even in the very place where they are appointed to find him. Or, as in dark nights, pirates used to kindle fires and make great lights upon the rocks and maritime coasts; whether, when the poor seaman steers, in hope of harbor, he meets with nothing but wrack and ruin. So, heretics flourish with Scriptures, or at least with some flashes of it, like false lights, to which when distressed souls repair for succor, these pestilent seducers feed them with nothing but pernicious errors. Fowlers, by setting up a dead tree smeared with lime and beset with dead birds, as if they were living, allure the live birds to them, as to their friends and acquaintances, and so bring them destruction. The application is easy; the experiments too common. Dead errors are made snares for living souls.

This is the cunning of these wicked impostors, something they will have good, to draw down the evil, the greater part shall be evil to poison the good. Gregory says in his *morals*: *Miscent recta perversis, ut oftendendo bona auditores adse pertrahant, et exhibendo mala, latenti peste corrumpant*. They seem saints at a distance and speak well, if you may believe them, but if you approach near to them and make a narrower discovery of them, you will find they are in sheep's clothing. If Rome did not have some truth, she would never be believed; if she were not full of errors, her followers could not be deceived. As the apostles from God, so the faithful ministers of God, from the apostles by the commandment of God, do warn us of these things so that we did not fall into the error of the wicked. It may be that we slight them speaking, but they of whom they warn us would give much to have them hold their peace. You know the story of *Philip* of Macedon besieging Athens, who sent legates to the city that if they would deliver into his hands ten of their orators, such as he should choose, whom he pretended to be disturbers of the common-wealth, he would raise his siege and be at peace with them. But *Demosthenes* quickly smelled out his plot and with the consent of Athenians, returned him this apological answer. The wolves came to treat of a league with the shepherds and told them in this way: *All the fraud and discord between you and us arises from a certain generation of dogs, which you maintain among you. Deliver up those dogs, and we will be good friends with you; neither will we in any way wrong you.* The dogs were delivered up; the peace was concluded; the shepherds secure. But, O, the woeful and cruel massacre that was presently made among the poor lambs; they were all devoured, the shepherds undone, and all by parting with the dogs. If the popish and schismatic faction, who like Samson's foxes are joined together by the trials, though their heads seem to be different one from the other, could once get the ministers of the Gospel to hold their peace or procure them to be muzzled by authority, or to be delivered over to their wolvish cruelty, woe to our poor souls. Error would then play havoc; darkness triumph; hell makes play-days; truth would languish; and all goodness would lay prostrate on the earth. As little as they are now regarded, or as much as they are slighted; we should then dearly miss them and earnestly wish for them, and say, blessed are they that come to us, not only in the name of the Lord, as most seducers do, but also sent from the Lord, to his glory and our establishment.

Let us then, while we do enjoy them, gather strength from them against vacillation and inconstancy. There are some of whom the apostle Paul speaks, "And they shall turn away their ears from the truth, and shall be turned unto fables," (2 Tim. 4:4); *toys* will lead away fools. A new fashion does not take a proud lady (nor a new plaything your roaring gallant; a new tavern your deep drinker; a new trick your nimble cheater; a new drug your gulling pharmacist) anymore than a new opinion takes your light-headed schismatic. Christ questions the Jews, "What went ye out in the wilderness to see? A reed shaken with the wind?" (Matt. 11:7). Yes, rather, O, you reeds shaken in the wind, what did you go out to the wilderness to see? A vanity lighter than yourselves? Yet as the golden calf which the Israelites made because their earrings, so a fictitious conceit transports too many among us because it is made fit for their ears.

Let us truly weight the folly of inconstancy, "Be not carried about with divers and strange doctrines: for it is a good thing that the heart be established with grace; not with meats, which have not profited them that have been occupied therein," (Heb. 13:9); to be loose then in the main joints of religion is very bad. The tottering wall is soon blown down, but being down, who will erect and set it up again? The righteous souls is like a body of a square figure; turn it on which part you will, lay it how you like, it will still be constant and like itself. An unstable Christian is the world's worst movable; slightly resembling a silk-worm, but not of such profit. One day you will find him a fly, another a maggot, very seldom twice in the same shape. Take gold and throw it into the water, yet it loses neither value nor color, cast it into the fire, and it comes forth purer; but dirt is hardened with the fire and dissolved in the water. The sons of levity are such, as that which they are joined withal would have them to be: hard or soft, cold or hot, tall or low, great or small, of any temper. Their souls are like common strumpets; they take in all suggestions. If one says there is no hell, they believe it. If another will come and say that there is no heaven, no angel, or no God, they are apt to be taken with it. For shame let us be steady before we are laid in the steady earth, where there is no motion at all. In the grave the most pragmatic busybody will be quiet. There is no shifting of ground, no changing of sides there. They that trouble all the country with their fantastical opinions, to get themselves a name, will lie there as quiet as their fellow clods. The body shall be confined to one place, the soul to another, without shifting or removing, until the time comes that they are removed to the bar and brought before the tribunal of the Lord Jesus, to receive *secundum opera*, according to their works.

I confess that we are sheep, apt to wander, but we will not if we keep to our Shepherd. We are chickens apt to stray, but we may be secure under the wings of our Hen. God is our Shepherd; let us keep close to him; never did any trust in him and miscarry. The holy Catholic Church is the hen under whose wings we have been hatched, let us carefully brood ourselves under the same, from the danger of the kite. Let us keep in the one and depend upon the other by our faith and prayers; and all the forces of Satan will not remove us from the truth. Which God of his mercy grant we may to his glory, our own comfort, and the good example of others. *Amen*

FINIS.[3]

[3] There is an excellent piece of the same author's work against the Socinians with a history of their lives and deaths. It has not been published for 400 years.

www.ingramcontent.com/pod-product-compliance
Lightning Source LLC
LaVergne TN
LVHW051009080826
845145LV00009B/2537
9781626630550